Innermost Thoughts of a Poet

Poems & Illustrations by
Samuel M. Dickerson

Copyright © 2024 by

Samuel M. Dickerson

ALL RIGHTS RESERVED. No part of this book may be reproduced or transmitted in any form by any means, electronic or mechanical, including photocopying and recording, or by any information storage and retrieval system, except as may be expressly permitted in writing from the author.

Printed in the United States of America

Acknowledgments

First, I'd like to thank God for every blessing He's given me, every test He's put me through, and most of all, for all the special people He put into my life. I thank God for the ability to express my thoughts, emotions, and life experiences. Thank you, God.

Second, I'd like to thank all my children for inspiring me to want to be a better father and a good role model. I want to be someone that y'all will look up to besides God. I want to inspire y'all to do great things. Believe me when I say that if I could do it, so can you! And I'm not just talking to my children. I'm talking to the youth worldwide.

To my first love, I love you. And my second love, I love you too. It's the both of you that made me love as deeply as I do. I wrote a series of love poems as dedications so you can see exactly what you meant—and still mean—to me. I know I wasn't the greatest guy in the past. I was young and did not know how to appreciate a good woman when I had one. And while our relationships came to an end, you both gave me the timeless gift of experiencing and learning about true love. For that, I am forever grateful. If I ever find love again, I'm going to cherish it and never let it go.

I would like to thank the people who caused me pain because my struggles have only made me stronger. I would also like this poetry book to serve as an apology to all the people I hurt, mistreated, or let down in the past. I'm sorry and hope you will forgive me.

I would like to thank all my family members, friends, and loved ones. I would like to acknowledge the people who touched my life in so many ways, such as my mother, my brother, my dad, my nana, my grandmothers, and my other family members who are in Heaven watching over me. I would also like to thank my children's mothers for raising my children and being great mothers to them. Thank you.

I would like to thank all my supporters who purchased my first book, *Inspirational Quotations*, and have given me feedback and the confidence to continue writing and take on my next challenge, the editing and publication of *Innermost Thoughts of a Poet*. Thanks a lot! I really appreciate every one of you. I couldn't have done it without you. I wish you many blessings.

I'd like to thank Dr. May for always being a good listener and offering not only constructive criticism on all my projects (such as my books) but also for giving me great advice and helping me in every way that she has. Thanks for seeing something in me when I couldn't see what I had been capable of doing all along. I have nothing but love, respect, and admiration for you. I couldn't have done it without you. I appreciate you and wish you many blessings.

To all my readers: Thank you for allowing me to walk you through the valleys of my mind, heart, and soul. In many ways, my poetry book is an autobiography. All the poems I wrote are from my life experiences, thoughts, trials, and tribulations. Most of all, they come from the heart. I kept them simple enough for everyone to understand and digest. They are not perfect, just like I am not perfect. But I hope you will be able to relate to them and see yourself in them. I hope they will be inspiring. Please read them, share them, and enjoy them.

God bless you.

Samuel H. Dickens

Table of Contents

Part V: Poems of Motivation and Inspiration for the Next Generation 325

Part I:
My Life Journey in Poems: From Tribulation to Triumph

Once Upon a Time

Once upon a time, before my life of crime began

I was just one of many innocent kids trying to emulate what I saw

Searching for my purpose in life and unlocking closed doors

Once upon a time, before I knew anything about crime

You could see my innocence written all over my face

I was so young and eager to learn

I couldn't wait until I grew a little taller

I had plans even as a child, playing with my toys in my bathwater

I remember saying when I get older, *I'm going to change the world*

And singing my little heart out at every opportunity I was given

I never imagined myself being in psychiatric centers, jails, or prisons

I thought I was clairvoyant, but I really couldn't see life from a distance

I grew up watching people get high off of crack, weed and coke

And if it wasn't drugs in the air, it was clouds of cigarette smoke

Circling the rooms, I'd visit

But like a good ole boy, I learned at a young age to go mind my own business

Once upon a time, I was taught that boys do the outside work and girls do the dishes

Once upon a time, my life was somewhat vicious

My Blood, Sweat, and Tears

I feel as if I've been blessed with not only a gift to converse and give God glory

But also the ability to incorporate my blood, sweat, and tears into each and every one of my poetical stories

I speak of life, liberty, love, as well as the Heavens above while attempting not to judge

Because who am I, but one of many given life

I also recognize the lost souls desperately searching for crumbs, screaming, *I had enough*

I know what it feels like to wake up with hunger pains in the middle of the night

And to reside in a house or building filled with rats, flies, roaches, and mice

That crawl-up bedroom, bathroom, living room, and kitchen walls

Searching for food like they're so cool

And paying rent to live with you

Just the thought alone is enough to make someone feel miserable

For those that can actually relate, tell me if what I'm saying isn't up to date

Mice'll try to hide wherever they can

Your cereal box'll have roaches even when you don't let them in

The rats'll eat through your sheetrock at times

The flies'll annoy you when you try to sleep

They'll also try to lay eggs on you

And enjoy anything they see you eat

When I Was 9 Years Old

When I was nine years old, I got hit by a car

I woke up inside the hospital with pins inside my legs

I spent one year in the hospital

I couldn't get up and go to the bathroom when I wanted to

I had a urinal and bedpan next to my bed

Both of my legs were broken, and I was in serious pain

I took medication sometimes when the pain wouldn't go away

The pins used to slide from side to side through my bones

I'd scream at the doctor, *You're doing this for your own pleasure!*

When he tried to align the pins

I have been in a wheelchair

I walked with a walker

I know how it is

I can relate to using crutches

Because at one point in time

My life did feel disgusting

Faith

I got hit by a car, and I don't remember it

But when I woke up, I had both of my legs in the air

I was trying to get out of my hospital bed

But what I didn't realize is I had pins in my legs

I was in pretty bad shape

I don't even remember the day

All I know is I had just recently turned nine

The next day, I remember the doctor coming into my room

Telling me there's a possibility I'd never be able to walk again

As soon as I heard the doctor say that

I silently spoke to God, and I remember saying,

I know you're going to let me walk again

That was almost 40 years ago

And you know what?

All I had was faith

And all I have is faith now

If you're having a problem, go to God

Let God hear your prayer

And most of all, have faith in God

Because God can work miracles

If He did it for me

He'll do it for you too

The First Time

The first time I tried weed, I was fourteen years old

The reason I tried it was because I wanted to be grown

After taking a couple of tokes, I decided I didn't like it

Because it was something that I didn't find very enticing

And besides, I already knew without being told

That I could do a whole lot better if I kept my thoughts together

It didn't take me forever to strategize a game plan

And it wasn't because of fear, either

I told myself I'm not gonna become an addict to no reefer

The Streets

The streets turned me into someone I didn't want to be

The person I became wasn't really me

It was just an illusion

Someone caught up in all the confusion

Living from one day to the next

Hustling to get someone else's check

I was the person who wanted everyone's respect

I didn't care whether I lived or died

I didn't think I'd make it to be 18 years of age

I was moving at a very fast pace

And I had no intention of slowing down

I learned how to cook up drugs, distribute drugs

I hung around thugs, pimps and players

And women who were only attracted to gangsters

I learned a lot about life from just being observant

I even learned from individuals

Who had the characteristics of serpents

They kept me on my toes

Some of my greatest allies started out as my foes

What tomorrow will bring, only God knows

I just pray I never experience any more dark roads

Because my life has already been Hell as it is

I just want to build a brighter future for my family, friends,

And especially my kids

People, Places, and Things

People, places and things'll get you in trouble

I grew up tossing bricks

I come from a very poor household

Where everyone's taught how to hustle

My mother would always run out of money

Because she'd always have to put food in the refrigerator

For me and my siblings

Life was really rough

It's hard trying to cope

When you barely have enough

I grew up fast

I hung around hustlers

It was either you were the seller or you were the customer

When the crack epidemic hit, that was all she wrote

Everybody and their mamma was playing cutthroat

Trying to get a little paper

Even if it meant selling drugs to their neighbors

For the sacrifices I made, God forgive me

The life I lived was risky

The only thing on my mind was the hundreds, twenties and fifties

I Feel Compelled

I feel compelled to tell my story and open the eyes of the infidel

You'll either love me or hate me after you hear my tale

Growing up was so real for me, and mines

I felt like I had to commit crimes just to survive

I sold poison to my own people just to get by

And laughed while they were getting high

Because, at the time, I wasn't interested in a nine-to-five

Selling poison was all I knew

A new shirt on my back, a new pair of jeans

And a pair of sneakers was like a dream come true

I was living the life of a poor man's dream

Or so it seemed, trying to get mine by any means

I thought I'd never get knocked with rocks inside my jeans

And a pocket full of leaves

Until that day came, I never thought it would be me

The system shattered my dreams

And now I'm paying the price

All my sudden mishaps caused me to make changes in my life

And stop playing with dice

After years of living in the dark, it's like that light switch finally turned on

And now, every day, I wake up feeling as if I've been reborn

Can U Relate?

Nobody knows how it feels to be me

If only others were able to see some of the things I saw

Or suffer the consequences I endured

Then, people could understand what prompted me to break the law

Can you relate to how hideous life feels being poor

Or having to drink powdered milk, eat government cheese

And wear the same pair of jeans to school two or three times a week?

Have you ever felt like you needed to see a shrink

Or told yourself, *My life smells worse than a skunk's*

Or felt so down you thought you'd never be able to climb out of the slums?

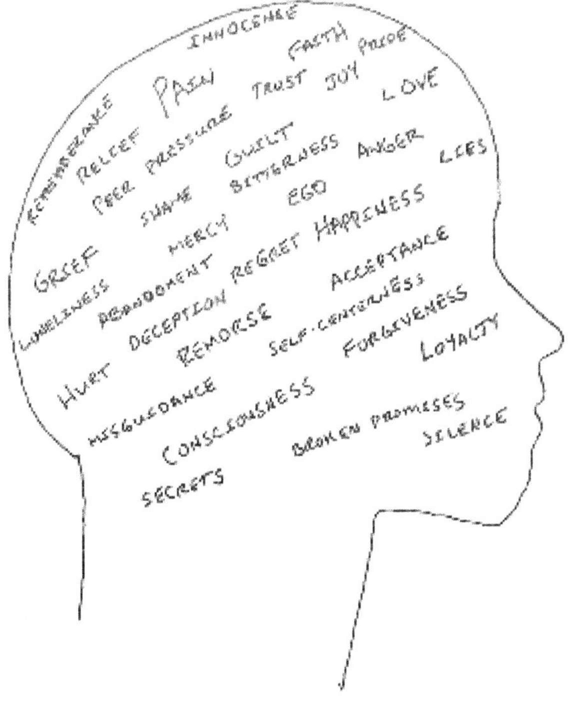

Counterproductive Thoughts

I beat myself up in the past

Whenever things didn't go my way, I'd spazz out

Sometimes, I felt like my whole world came crashing down

Without me even being aware

I was in the streets, but I moved like a square

I learned the hard way life isn't always fair

I thought I had it all figured out, but I really wasn't prepared

For all life had to offer

Growing up on welfare

Made me feel like I was being tortured and strangled

It seemed like every time I turned around

Life was coming at me from another angle

Sometimes, I felt like I was being brainwashed

I used to constantly ask myself when this locomotive train would stop

All the stress had me feeling as if my head was gonna pop

Still, I tried to stay one step ahead

Away from any counterproductive thoughts

The Past

I've been misled – some things were, and some things weren't said

I've been deceived – there are some things I should never have believed

I've been led astray – although they tell me there'll be better days

All I ever do is hope for the best

All I ever do is cope with the stress

All I ever do is prepare for whatever comes next

I guess it wasn't always in my best interest to take others' advice

A lot of things I learned came with a high price

The sacrifices I made just to get a pair of Nikes and a nice coat

I grew up playing cutthroat – when cars came, we all ran

Who's the first to get served

I'm familiar wit the block, and I really stood on the curb

Hanging out all night trynta get to the bag

Pockets full of coins made my jeans sag

Toxic work sometimes got the friends mad

I'd put the powder in the Pyrex, then made it play freeze tag

Nowadays, I wash my hands clean with Purell

Can you relate to them days or the way that chicken used to smell?

I remember how my life felt like when it was pure Hell

Nobody's Listening

As I stare into the eyes of my inner being

I realize he longs to be released

The heart of a man, the instinct of a beast

Constantly striving to find peace and fighting a battle that never ceases to amaze me

I wake up every day and ask myself, *Why's my life so crazy?*

What can I do to change the direction that I've been heading in for so many years?

I want to cry, but I'm all out of tears

I want to scream because I hate this life I'm living

But what sense would it make if nobody's really listening?

Who cares about my problems or how much pain I endure?

With nowhere else to turn, I petition the Lord

I Wanted to Be

I wanted to get paid

I wanted to get laid

I wanted a big chain

I wanted a nice car

I wanted hundreds and fifties and twenties

I wanted it so bad I even sold dummies

I wanted a wife, but I wasn't willing to stop cheating

I wanted what Scarface wanted: money, power, and respect

I wanted some of everybody else's check

I wanted a place to rest my head

I wanted a decent, comfortable bed

I wanted to absorb knowledge from all my teachers

I wanted to be just like hustlers, players, and pimps

I wanted to be someone known for using my wits

I wanted to leave the game alone when I chose to call it quits

I wanted to be the one that learned all the tricks of the game

I wanted to be the boy with all the brains

Now, I want to be the one who learns from his mistakes

Once I Start, I Don't Stop 'Til I'm Finished

Inmates and convicts battle convictions

Addicts battle addictions

This world is full of decisions

I speak, but nobody listens

I search for doors from a distance

The ways of Muslims and Christians

Of Hebrew slaves and Egyptians

And some folks who think they're magicians

I study, and Jehovah bears witness

And once I start, I don't stop 'til I'm finished

My Word and Money Issues

In a world where all you have is your word

And a few dollars to get by

I can't see why people make broken promises

And use their funds to get high

Even if I were penniless, I'd still try

To scrape up some nickels, dimes, and dollars

Because you never know what to expect from tomorrow

This world is strong enough

To make the most enthusiastic man's heart hollow if you let it

That's why when I don't get it, I don't sweat it

And when I tell somebody I will, I do

Even though sometimes that's not always true

Because sometimes things come up

But something I won't do

Is let my words or money issues leave me feeling blue

Nightmares I Share

These nightmares I share with the audience of my choosing

Tends to get folks upriled and cause mass confusion

Even when I'm not in a vehicle, it's like I'm cruising

While I'm wide awake, it feels like the world must be snoozing

I'm driving down the highway of my choice

Can you feel the power as it radiates from my voice?

If I were to stop talking, you'd still hear the echoes

I'm built like a black panther, and I move like a gecko

I'm coming and going, and I ain't even got a Metro card

My name rings bells like Pablo Escobar's

If you could gaze into my heart, you'd see a *boucoup* of scars

All my life, all I ever did was go against the odds

Life dealt me bad hands, so I learned how to switch the cards

I could live to be one hundred, and I'll still never forget my mom

I never had a license, but I drove plenty of rental cars

And had my own too

I'm one of them cool cats that's from the old-school

My Life Was Kinda Like a Matinee

My life was kinda like a matinee

I had some good days and some bad days

I was trapped between a rock and a hard place on some different occasions

But uncertainty caused me to glance at my past on an everyday basis

And peer through my binocular lens of life like I was given a new set of eyes

Now I realize I wasn't always the one that was in the right

And yes, sometimes I'll admit I did things out of spite

Like rile people up and watch as they'd fight one another

Because I was eager to see who really possessed the heart of thunder and who didn't

I figured that was be the best way for me to separate the lions from the chickens

Searching for Signs

As I gaze into the sky, searching for signs

I find none, not one single one

Yet I'm filled with love for my Father above

I made many mistakes, so who am I to judge

The Crips, Bloods, Trinitarios, Latin Kings, or white supremacists

When everyone is just trying to get in where they could fit in

But the cars are jam-packed

Riots occur while civilians stand back and watch

What's the sense of having a Million Man March

When the violence just doesn't stop?

Like crabs in a barrel, we're all eager to get to the top

And sometimes innocent people end up becoming someone they're really not

How it is Inside

The food sucks, but I eat to survive

I could tell you stories about how it is inside

Jails, prisons, and psychiatric centers

I walked down the roads so I can bear witness

Lights out after the final count

Your wife or girlfriend's cheating got you ready to start wildin' out

Every day, there's a discrepancy, somebody overly vexed

Fist fights and bullying everywhere you go

Because you told someone, *No*

If you ask me, everybody's just putting on a show

Arguments constantly occur just because you say how you feel

If you don't like the hand you're dealt, you better learn how to deal

Drugs on the gallery being smoked and sniffed

COs bring in the dogs, it's a hit or miss

Watch towers and rubber bullets just in case a riot breaks out

Pay attention to your surroundings because anyone's liable to pull a shank out

If you don't want to be labeled a snitch, you better learn to be quiet

Collect calls being rejected, enough to set you on fire

Mothers and wives are being harassed and turned away

And told today is not your son's or daughter's visiting day

Convicts walk the yards and lift weights in the cold

While eagerly waiting for their day to go home

No One's Perfect

On the surface, everything seems to be intact

Underneath the surface, everyone has cracks

Sometimes, you'll see mouths full of filth, deceit, envy and greed

Other times, you'll find the love that makes a hopeless man feel complete

Many deny their true motives

We're all made up of multiple components

I find there is love, life and wisdom in words

While others don't necessarily have to concur

Many seek knowledge, but only a few find it

I myself choose to be mindful and never be blinded

Once upon a time, I resorted to becoming violent

But now I'm learning how to walk away and remain silent

I let my arousers push me in the past

Now, I look at life through an unorthodox hourglass

While searching for my true purpose

I realize no one on Earth is perfect

This

This is what I call history in the making

I'm searching for answers and trying to find explanations

This is what I call a story of a hustler with nothing left to lose

I lost everything, but somehow, I managed to keep my shoes

This I what I believe will set me free

If I take away all my anger and let it flee

This is how I feel deep down within

I've been backstabbed so many times

I can't tell my foes from my friends

I don't know if I'll ever trust people again

This is one of the things I feel I need

Someone who'll stick by my side and love me just for being me

This is just another chapter of my life, and some of what I see

I wonder if Heavenly Wings is written in my destiny

Invisible Enemy

At times I feel like my life

Is being sucked right out of me

And I have a pair of invisible hands

Wrapped around my throat

And an inner voice whispering,

Just let go

As if I don't already know

What's in store for me

If I decide to travel down those roads

I impatiently traveled down before

Which nearly destroyed everything I touched

And left me feeling as if my mind was deteriorating

And my skull was being crushed

By an invisible enemy

Whom I knew I could never succumb to

Or trust

I Realize

I used to feel like I had it all: the money, the cars, the broads

But I failed to realize that my Earthly possessions

Were pulling me away from God

The more I obtained, the less pure my heart became

I guess you could say I fell victim to the marijuana, crack, and cocaine

And before I realized what was happening, I ended up getting sucked into the game

Every day, I woke up with the same thoughts on my mind

Stack my paper and perfect my grind

Now I realize how foolish I truly was

Because nothing worthwhile came from me selling drugs

I Struggled with Addiction

Many years ago, I struggled with addiction

My thoughts, as well as my behavior, were both unpredictable

I couldn't stop using

No matter how hard I tried

I was conscious of my external self

But wasn't ready to face my demons inside

Like many others

I thought I had it all figured out

Now, looking back in the mirror at the reflection of my past

I realize I was just like you

Smoking marijuana and cigarettes and drinking brews

To cope with the situations I faced

Or trying to find a solution

To deal with the problems

I wasn't ready to embrace

And the pain I couldn't erase

Now I wake up and tell myself every day

In order to make my future brighter

I can't repeat those same mistakes

Mistakes ◆ Regrets

There are some mistakes I made that I wish I could change

There are some regrets I have that I'd like to forget

But you know what I believe:

Everything happens for a reason

That's something I learned to admit

So, I guess I was meant to make these mistakes

Because all they did was make me stronger

I guess it was meant for me to live with the regrets I live with

Because it's the regrets

That stop me from repeating some errors

Have you made any mistakes?

Or do you have any regrets you live with?

It's just something to think about

What weighs heavily on your spirit?

I Gave Life All I Had

I can't blame you if you hate me

I'm deeply troubled, I must admit

Although I try to be humble and stick to the script

I'm too quick to forget when trouble arises

I'm a man of many disguises

I fall short day after day

I repent and constantly pray

And yes, every time I'm wrong

I also pay the price of life's faults and mistakes

I'm full of regrets

I just really wish I knew

When to use my brakes

And also do less

I gave life all I had to give

Since I was just a kid

But who am I kidding?

The turns I took were somewhat hidden

The mistakes I've made

Turned me into the man I became

I can be as sharp as a razor blade

Or as dumb as a sloth trying to cross the street

In a hundred-degree heat

Instead of doing the most

I should have been doing the least

Non-Fiction

I can smell fear from a mile away

I also have the ability to look someone in their eyes

And see if they're telling me the truth or lying to me

I was born with a sixth sense

I'm not the kind you'll ever have to convince

Sometimes, I listen to others while they lie

And I let it slide

You probably don't know, but I'll tell you why

I like to see how far people go

I like to listen to them tell me things

They think I don't already know

I'm kinda like a magician

And when people talk

I just pay attention

These words I speak are non-fiction

Poured It On

Some poured it on, and I thought knowledge was being born

I fell in love with the game and immediately said, *Mi amor*

Most of what I learned I could've bought from a dollar store

I wasn't athletic, and I had no desire to play basketball

But still, I knew I had skills

From the second I picked up a pen

I knew I'd let my message spill

Onto the paper

I have a mind like Einstein and the heart of a gangsta

But who am I to boast?

I ride till wheels fall off, and ain't no spokes

A lot of folks threw in the towel

I gave 'em hope

From a very young age

I knew how to cope

Keep Going

I'm learning how to adjust to not having much

But it's taking some time to get used to

I'm also being mindful of the bumps in the road

Because sometimes it seems crucial

I used to feel like I had a heart made of stone

And trust alone made me go cuckoo

I felt like life kept hitting me with low blows

And that was something I wasn't used to

I couldn't see much because I had my eyes closed

Once upon a time, I felt hopeless

But now I have my eyes open, and my mind's focused

And my inner voice whispers, *Samuel, keep going*

Now I Know I Was Wrong

I used to get a kick out of watching people suffer

I sold drugs to others so I could buy nice things

Like gold, sneakers, clothes, chains and diamond rings

I was what you could call someone addicted to the finer things

Life had to offer

I'd spend money on lawyers, girls, and cars

I was once considered a hood star

My pockets stayed as fat as a bullfrog

I was fly, y'all

And the funny thing is, I ain't even have to try hard

It all came natural

While others were suffering, I was crackling like the jackal

Now I know I was wrong

And I admit my wrongdoing in my poems

Because I didn't do it before

Bottled Up Emotions

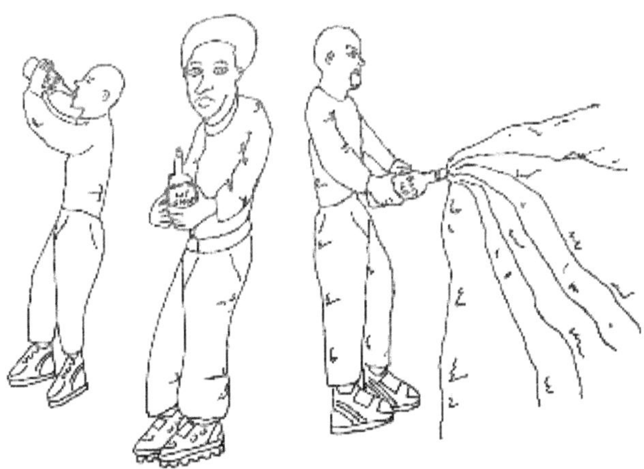

Instead of dealing with the issues in my life

I bottled up my emotions

And learned to hold onto the things that troubled me the most

Now, I'm learning how to let go

Little by little

And I see the difference it's making

Not only in myself but in those around me as well

I wish my mom was here so I could tell her

I never meant to put her through Hell

As those changes take place in my life

I find myself compelled to share my story

With my family, friends and those around me

And I'm more conscious nowadays

That life isn't all about me

Intelligent ◆ Insane

I'm tired of being lonely

I miss having a life

I wake up every day and wish I had a wife

Yet I know I'm not ready to love anytime soon

I'm bleeding internally, and I don't know what to do

But it's my own fault I'm in the position I'm in

These past 13 years gave me a good whippin'

But I have a small head that's as hard as a rock

And once I get started, I don't know when to stop

A chip off the old block, I'm just like my pops

That's how I was raised

And how I survived

I'm kind of amazed

Some say I'm intelligent

Others call me insane

Eyes Wide Open

Go ahead, I don't got no time to be indulging

The only way I'm looking at life right now is with my eyes wide open

For many years, I held back silent tears

I felt like it made no sense to cry because who really cares?

Now I see life isn't always as clear as it appears

To climb to the top, I had to first find the stairs

There's so much I miss about living

Even though I'm practically free

It feels like I'm trapped inside a prison

I just want to be able to soar to new heights

Start all over again and live a new life

This Odyssey

I'm not certain how it all began

But what I do know is this odyssey has yet to end

I've met some good friends along the way

Along with some formidable rivals whose names I won't say

And I've come to find

As far as life and living goes

There's always more than what the eye is able to perceive

I live life like I'm in school, and each experience

It is just another class I take to get my degree

At my graduation ceremony, there won't be any phony smiles

Or envious pats on the back

Because the people who rooted for me

Will look me in my eyes

And they'll tell me they believed in me

And had faith that I'd survive

On Your Mark, Get Set, Get Ready, Let's Go

Life is strange, and it caused me to have some icy veins

I wake up, and I feel at a loss for words

Sometimes, I feel like my thoughts are disturbed

They call me crazy, but they can never say I'm lazy

My mind runs rapidly

I set a time, and afterward, I tap in

I don't do dental, I do mental extractions

And I cause global reactions

Poetry's my passion, as you probably already know

On your mark, get set, get ready, let's go

I Can See the Light

There's not a day that goes by when I'm not eagerly searching

For the light that shines within my soul

Sometimes, I think I found it; other times, it's like it doesn't glow

When all else fails, I get on my knees and pray for guidance, knowledge, wisdom and strength

And suddenly, I find myself revitalized at times when I feel weak

I'm beginning to look at the world with a new set of eyes

I can see straight through the smoke screens, disguises and lies

That once were unnoticeable to my Earthly lens

And I hear people's cries from psych centers and pens

As if their pain has slowly become my own

And now I realize I can take my problems to God

Because He's listening from His throne

And I share this story with the people

So they will know they're not alone

How I Feel

I'm not a perfect human being, and I have my own flaws, just like everyone else

You know what makes me different?

I analyze, adapt, and learn from my surroundings

And open up doors that would have remained shut

Had I not decided to change my lifestyle and stand up for what I believe in

Today, I find myself not only fighting for freedom

But also searching for the hidden treasure that lies within my soul

While trying to avoid insults, forks in the road, and the uncertainties of being alone

You see, we live in a world where life, sometimes, just isn't fair

Only experience can turn a girl into a woman and a boy into a man

When I exited the womb, I wasn't prepared for the lessons life had to offer

But now that I'm nurturing my mind

I realize life is just as gentle as a leaf blowing in the wind

And part of me wishes I could take back all the time I spent living recklessly

And start all over again

I Changed My Life

I take delight in the changes I've made in life

But like Christ, I pay the ultimate price of constantly being stoned

Like lingering pain in my bones

If you listen close enough, you can almost feel the pain in my poems

Bear with me as I sputter some of my thoughts and emotions

Of my past life, being redefined

By a man who looks at the world using more than just his third eye

To lead the deaf, mentally ill and blind

Instruction weighs heavily on my mind, and I use it as my guide

Although it overwhelms me at times

Because you see, these mountains I climb are taller than Mount Everest

And to find their whereabouts, I learned never to be a pessimist

Nor can I submit to the tribulations I encounter along the way

I made myself a promise that I'd never go astray

So I rise every day with one thought on my mind

Which is to love like I've been loved

And keep a heart full of hope and faith

While I wait on God to bestow me

With His Almighty Grace

Slow Me Down

They told me I'd never make it

And the craziest thing is I believed them

I told them I had dreams and goals I wanted to accomplish

Their exact words were, "Stop the nonsense!"

I've stopped using for over a decade

And I feel so much better

I guess they thought that I was going to use drugs forever

I'm clean and sober now

I try to watch my karma

Because I know what goes around

And I refuse to let a pessimistic thinker's thoughts

Slow me down

A Test and Testimony

Every day of life

Is something I see as not only a test

But as a testimony

Of the man I am, the man I was, and the man I will be

I enjoy being me

Although sometimes it could be scary

I don't wear a cloak or put on a façade

What you see is what you get

What comes from my heart

That is exactly what's inside my heart

My originality sets me free

I stand in a class of my own

I don't need anyone else to get into the zone

Unlike a lot of other brothers

I'm far from a leech or any other bloodsuckers

And when it all boils down

I'll stand up for mines

Just like Rock against Tucker if I have to

Because being a protector

It is something that comes natural

Motivation

They laughed at me – when I told them I would make it

But that's what I expected – because they barely believed in themselves

So I used their laughter as fuel – to motivate me even further

I can't give up, I won't give up – that's what I kept telling myself

Second after second, minute after minute, hour after hour

Day after day, week after week, month after month, year after year

I told myself I would be successful

If it's not today – it'll be tomorrow

If I keep hope alive and continue to strive – someday, I'll shine

Like stars in the sky – or fireworks on the 4th of July

Eventually, my time will come – like a warm summer sun

So there's really no need to rush – to get to my destination

I have a vision like an artist with nothing – but a canvas, brushes, and dedication

What I Believe

Every time I pick up my pen and grab a hold of a piece of paper

I feel as if I'm just one of many strangers trying to express what I do best

Preparing to share another one of my tales with a hostile world

I have so many topics to choose from

By the time tomorrow comes, I'll already have new ones brewing

If I'm not part of the problem, I must be part of the solution

Who knows what I'm actually doing

Besides jotting down some of my inner thoughts

While I choose to talk about life

Others are focused on sports

However, in this arena, there's only room for one teacher

I'm what you call a poet and a hood preacher

An artist and entrepreneur

I can see great things occurring in my future and

Although most of my tales have some rhyme

The only thing I'm trying to do is find the door to the other side

In my next life, I'll probably come back as a butterfly or an angel

Jesus said if you truly believe, all things are able

A Sculptor ☆ An Artist ☆ A Dreamer

I sculpt out of clay, paper, aluminum and soap

I do so with the hope that I can

Bring what is once considered nothing to life

It makes me feel good to be able to create something

And give it to someone

I hope someday to become a professional sculptor

Make toys for children worldwide

And see how many smiles

I can put on their faces

I don't really know how to use tools when I sculpt

But it's only because I never tried, I guess

I mold from the substances I named

And bring figurines to life

My mother taught me how to sculpt out of clay and flour

I taught myself how to sculpt out of aluminum, soap and paper

I'm an artist

That's what an artist does

Takes nothing and turns it into something

Just because

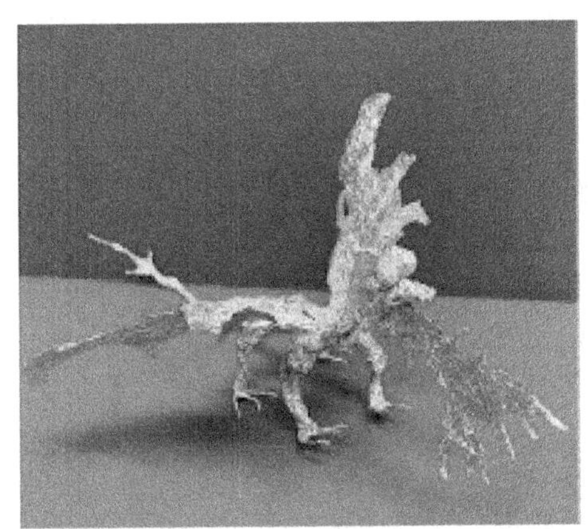

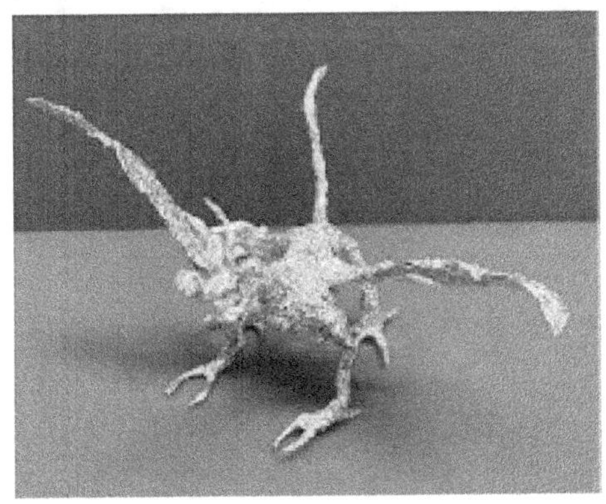

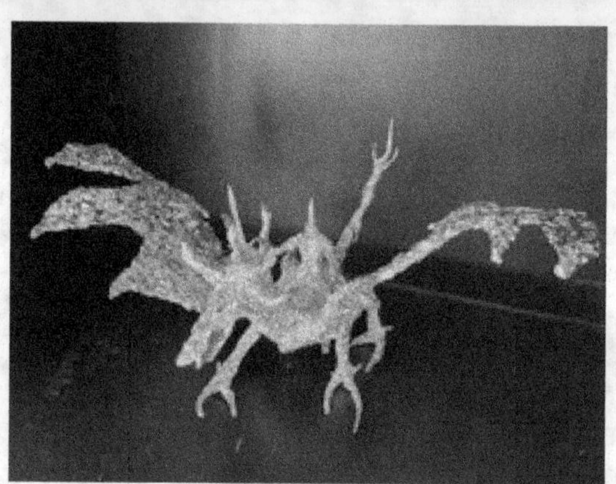

What I Am

I'm not just a poet, I'm a sculptor

I'm an inventor, I'm a musician

I'm a hustler and an entrepreneur

I'm a child of God, I'm a father

I'm a brother, I'm an uncle

And I'm a grandfather,

I'm a risk taker, I'm a survivor

I'm a go-getter, I'm a chess player

I'm a friend to my friends

I'm a God-fearing man

I'm the master of my own destiny

My Synopsis

I'm just another brother who chooses to tell his story

My synopsis revolves around pain, knowledge, shame, grit, and glory

I'm just a lonely soul searching for enlightenment

Traveling down a path that can be somewhat frightening

When I'm long gone, my literature will live on forever

My only hope is that the pictures I paint will always be remembered

I tell the tales of the lost generation

I pray that someday, others can see beneath the surface

And find better ways to take out their frustrations

Sometimes, I feel like the world is nothing but a circus

Full of actors and clowns

Making people laugh and smile

Trying to perform as best we can

Before our day finally comes

To lie down and pay the price for all of our sins

You're You, and I'm Me

We don't dress alike

We don't sound alike

We don't write alike

We don't dance alike

We don't romance alike

We don't love alike

We don't look alike

We don't sing alike

Because we're not alike

You're you, and I'm me

I have desires, so I chase my dreams

I also know there's no one like me

I'm a poor man filled with hope

This is just one of the ways I choose to cope

Whether writing poems or uttering notes

This is just the path of life I chose

A Scientist

Now, let's see where I should start

I grew up putting things back together

After I had already taken them apart

I was eager to find out why everything worked

The way they worked

I wanted to know why everything had a purpose

For being placed exactly where it was placed

I was a scientist at heart

From the second I was given life

The most dominant thought in my mind

Was, *Why, why, why, why?*

I learned through trial and error

How to look at life clearer

Yet, some things I learned

Made me avoid looking at myself in a mirror

Nothing about me is perfect

Above or underneath the surface

But what I can say truthfully

Is that I am soul-searching

God's Support

It's been over 13 years since I last smoked or drank

I feel so much better; now my eyes aren't redder

I'm able to think clearly, and I have a great sense of direction

Though I'll admit the dots just really started connecting

I see myself doing better in the future

I'm expecting a marvelous outcome once I'm done

And I can finally say no more alcohol or drugs

My days of marijuana and cigarettes are through

I'm tired of walking in a pair of shoes that just don't fit

It's time I changed the script

I decided to place my troubles in the Lord's hands and let Him fix me

I'm not saying I'm perfect because there's parts of my life that are still iffy

Because I still fall short

But I know I can manage and overcome

With God's divine support

Peace

Peace, my brothers of many mothers

Peace, my mothers and fathers from yonder

Peace, my friends and neighbors of all flavors

Peace, I say, even to my rivals

This love I have is not just tribal

The love I have extends to the end of the Earth

I love others even when love begins to hurt

I'll travel that extra mile to make my friends smile

Or donate a piece of myself to save someone else

When I love, there's no limitation involved

My love's like a bomb when unleashed

It doesn't only explode

It reloads as I speak

And shines as bright as gold

While warming the heart of the cold

Internally, I found the peace

That fills up my soul

Some Days

Some days are unpredictable

Some days, I feel like nothing could go wrong

Some days, I wake up and take a half hour in the shower

Some days, I don't take that long

Some days, I eat my breakfast and enjoy it

Some days, I'm just not in the mood to eat, so I don't destroy it

Some days, I wake up and tell myself I wish I could go back to sleep

Some days, it feels like all I ever do is think

Some days, I'm motivated

Some days, I'm not

Some days, I wonder why I'm not already on top

Some days, I want to work

Some days, I just feel like being lazy

Some days, I look in the mirror and feel as if I'm going crazy

Some days, people call me

Some days, people are too busy

Some days, I wonder who truly misses me

Some days, I ask myself, *Am I on the verge of making history?*

Be Grateful

Life's a gamble, and sometimes you lose, sometimes you win

There's really no telling what'll actually transpire each day

You just gotta be ready for whatever comes when it comes

One of the most valuable lessons I learned in life

Is to always count my blessings and make the most of the opportunities I've been given

So nowadays, instead of complaining about what I don't have

I learned to appreciate everything I have

And not to take even the smallest things for granted

Such as friendships, my children, my loved ones, my family

Because everything is a gift from God

I value the air I breathe, the meals I receive

The shelter I'm given, no matter where I'm at

Because I know there's always someone else who's suffering more than me

And wish they had what I have

After years of always complaining

I learned to be grateful and content

For everything that I have and don't have

And everything that I get

Optimistic Thoughts

There are so many things I want to get off my chest

But I live with regrets and face each day optimistically

Mentally, emotionally, and physically

I don't see myself as a pessimistic thinker

It's been over 13 years since I've been a smoker and a drinker

I've been clean and sober, and I don't ever plan to relapse

That's why I'm preparing each and every day

I want to have structure in my life

And I want to be sober as I live life to the fullest

I want to travel around the world to other countries

Meet new people and build houses of worship and homeless shelters around the world

I want to take every talent God gave me and use it to help others

So they can live their lives better

I want to teach my children and the children that don't have parents

Nothing is impossible to do

If you set your mind towards getting things done

And I want the kids from the ghettos worldwide

To shine like the sun

Unfamiliar Jargon

Pardon my unfamiliar jargon

But I'm kinda like a lightning rod

Some knowledge I take in

The rest I discard

I'm not a scholar yet—at least not in my own eyes

Though I wish I were, at times

Which comes as no surprise

I realize everything has a meaning and purpose

But the wisdom I seek lies deep beneath the surface

I'm far from superficial

However, I shine brighter than crystals,

Diamonds and reflections in the mirrors

I weigh men and women on their deeds

Not on their appearance

The point I'm making is

I learned so much from the experience

And proud to say

I'm taking life serious

I'm Determined to Pass

If this is just a test, I'm determined to pass

I love you with all my heart; I learned from my past

The mistakes I made only made me stronger

With God on my side, I don't even need a lawyer

I wasn't always right, and I wasn't always wrong

I had good times, bad times, and random thunderstorms

However, every day, I try to live better

There are some parts of my life I wish I didn't remember

I'm eager to excel, but it feels like my time is taking forever

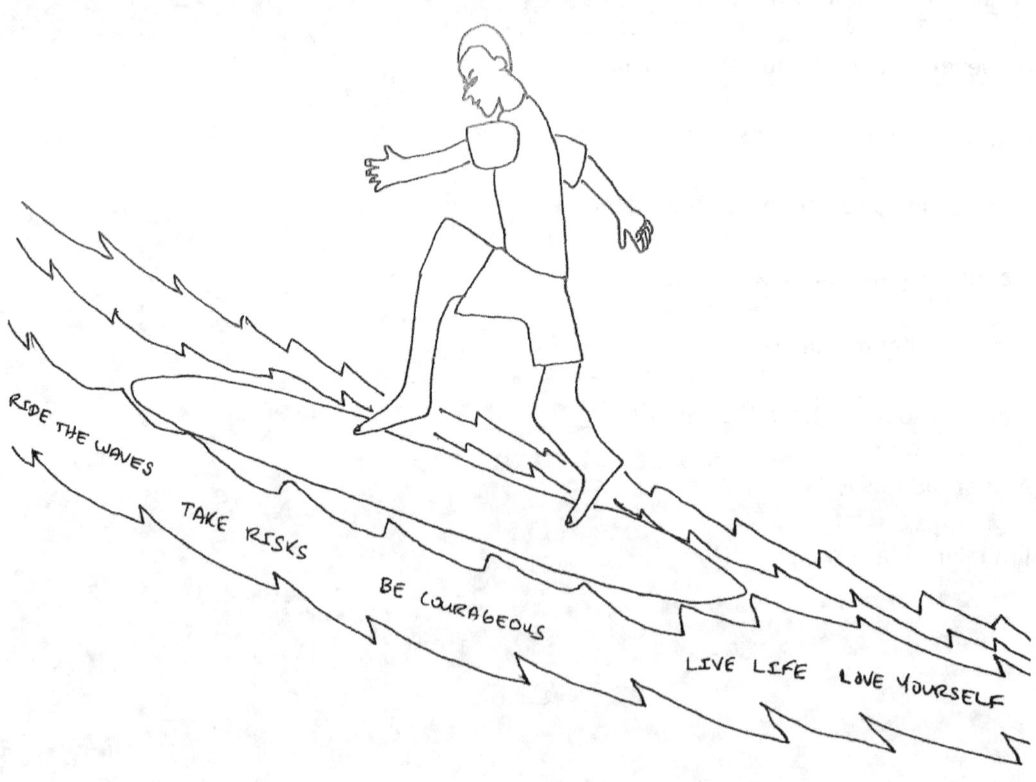

In the Near Future

I hope to really live life and enjoy each day

In the presence of my family, friends, and acquaintances, close and far away

In the near future

I hope to be financially secure

Because I'm tired of being poor

I hope to have enough wealth to build houses of worship and shelters for the homeless

In the near future

I hope to be a great example of someone who changed my life

So others can emulate my ways and live prosperous lives

In the near future

I hope I can find someone who loves me for me

And not for the things I have to offer them

In the near future

I hope to have more children so that I can teach them

The difference between right and wrong

In the near future

I hope to be called upon by God Himself

And given an assignment to carry out

In the near future

I hope to find my true soulmate

In the near future

I hope to become someone whose words of wisdom

Change the world

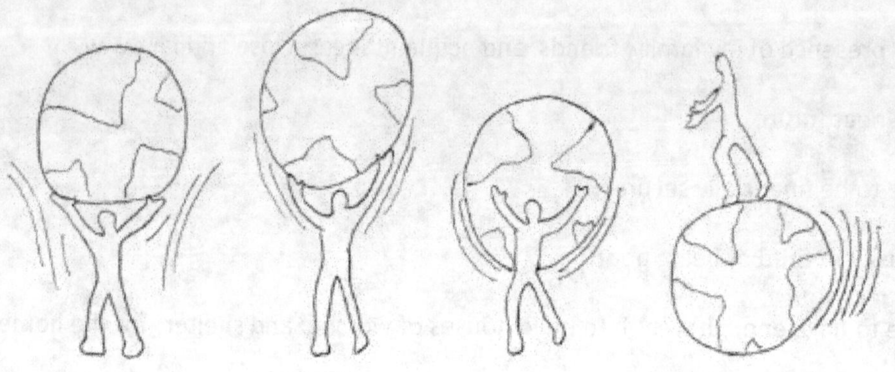

When I Make It Big

When I make it big

The first person I'm going to thank is God

Then I'm going to thank my mother and brother, even though they're in Heaven

Then, I'm going to thank my children for inspiring me to want to be a better father

Then I'm going to thank every one of my friends that believed in me

And told me I could do it

When I make it big

I'm going to thank my first love for being someone who showed me love and for teaching me what true love really is

When I make it big

I'm going to thank all my teachers, like Mr. Armstrong, for teaching me math

And Ariel and Dr. Heller for pushing me when I was ready to give up on myself

When I make it big

I'm going to thank my creative partner and confidant for also inspiring me, believing me and helping me accomplish my goals

When I make it big

I'm going to thank all the inmates, convicts, staff and patients I lived with for so many years for allowing me to tell their stories and my own

Riches Beyond Riches

I'm a wealthy man when it comes to mind, body, and spirit

I possess riches beyond riches

For I do not seek the wealth or wisdom of mortal men

Yet I have a heart made of gold, a platinum body

And a bronze mind

My spirit is made of silver lining

When I bleed, I bleed the blood of Jesus, my Lord and Savior

I walk the path of the straight and narrow

I consume the bread of life, and it nourishes me

I stand still, waiting for the arrival of my blessings

Plant Fruitful Seeds

I am nothing more than a sacrificial lamb

Searching for my true purpose in life

While being pursued by hyenas and wolves in sheep's clothing

I am a revolutionist and innovator of the present

As well as the future

This man, boy, or child you hear and *think* you know

Is only a reflection of the spirit that lies below

These words I speak so boldly

Arise from the depths of my soul

I speak in parables like my mentor,

Lord and Savior Jesus Christ

And when I crave knowledge and guidance

I turn to the Bible for advice

I seek emeralds and pearls

That are not of this world

So that one day, I may plant fruitful seeds

Inside the souls, hearts and minds

Of young boys and young girls

It's Painful to Watch

It's painful to watch single mothers struggling

And also to know there's really not much I can do to help

Besides offer words of encouragement

The same as I do to myself

To the mothers out there that need some inspiration

To all the mothers on welfare and all the mothers that are homeless

Just be patient

I see y'all struggling to make ends meet

I hope and pray someday to be successful

Because I want to help the less fortunate

I know how it feels to have to make sacrifices

To take care of your children

My mother did what she had to do

To take care of me and my siblings growing up

And watching her made me more resilient

And I just want to one day be able to give back to the world

For all I've taken

But for now, I'm just practicing being patient

And my blessings are right over the horizon

Like a rising sun

I'm waiting for my time to come

So I can teach this world

How to show genuine love

One Day

One day, I'm going to shine so bright

I'm going to put the sun to shame

And in my shadow, they'll be rays of light

One day, I'm going to find the girl of my dreams

And I'm going to look her in the eyes and tell her

I love you, sweetheart

And I'm going to get on one knee

And pull out a beautiful diamond ring and

Ask her, *Will you be mine forevermore?*

One day, I'm going to build houses of worship and

Homeless shelters for people who don't have anywhere to live

And would like to praise God

One day, I'm going to teach my children

That even though I have a mental illness

I didn't give up

And neither should they

Even More Resilient

Success doesn't come overnight

In order to get what you want out of life

You have to be willing to work hard, stand up and fight sometimes

Not only that, either—

You need to be determined

And also a true believer

It pays to have faith in someone greater

And I can honestly say that I love my Creator

I try not to question why life is the way that it is

But I am attempting to make life better for my friends, family and children

In order to reach my goals

I just keep on building

Whatever doesn't kill me

Only makes me resilient

FIGHT LIFE
WIT
ALL U GOT

My Calling in Life

All I need is a clean house, some home-cooked meals

A quiet place to sculpt and write my books, songs, and poetry

And a California King bed to rest my head

And I'll feel like the champion that I am

Then I'll probably sculpt and write all day and night

Because I not only enjoy sculpting and writing

But I love giving things substance that have no substance

I know I'm not God, and I can't compare to what He's capable of doing

However, I'm attempting to follow in His footsteps

He's my perfect example of how a person should be

By bringing something to life

It makes me feel like I found my calling

Learning to Love

I'm striving to become a better person

I'm constantly soul-searching

While the wheels keep turning

I want to be brilliant, resilient

And pave a better way for children

I'm eager to let my light shine and live a prosperous life

I want to be divine in all aspects

I'm not concerned with wealth, cars or jewelry

I would like to build up all of the broken communities

I would like for my words to be heard, felt, and appreciated by all

I think it's time we set aside our differences

And started learning to love each other a little more

I
LOVE
POETRY

I Want to Be Someone Who Helps

Pray for me and hope I reach my peak

I want to be someone who helps clean up the streets

I'd like to be someone capable of changing the world

And making it a better place to live in

I'm tired of seeing so many people suffer

And so much money spent on building prisons

And other kinds of institutions

I feel like if we have a problem

Then, we probably need to come together and find a solution

If we want change to take place

We gotta be like Nike and *just do it*

Or else we're always going to have issues

We need to refrain from our current ways

And stop resorting to the usage of missiles

Whenever we feel the need to engage

We need to reconstruct society

And stop being so vague

My Light

As I shine my light in the darkest places

I ask myself,

Shall I remain loquacious

And teach the world what it's never been taught

While fighting a fight that has never been fought?

I've learnt that words can be mightier than swords

Because they possess the power

To build or destroy nations

In the blink of an eye

So I constantly tell the youth worldwide

To swallow their pride

Chase their dreams

Reach for the sky

And most importantly,

Let God be their guide

Part II:
Poems of Gratitude:
To Those Who Touched My Life

Loved Ones

You know something,

Every moment I spend with my loved ones

Is a moment I cherish

I learned the hard way

Not to take advantage of the time

God gives me with my loved ones

Because tomorrow is not promised

I lost a lot of loved ones throughout the years

And I know I'll lose more in time

So I learned to make the most out of every second I'm given

With my loved ones

Because I know sometimes

I won't get a chance to say goodbye

Go On

Part of me feels like it's being tortured

The other half of me feels as if I'm discovering my greatest gift

I feel uplifted at times

Then sometimes, I start to feel down

Other times, I shift

I remind myself every day

I have to make my mother, brother, and father proud

I miss my loved ones,

I wish I could make them smile

So I write about them

And hold them in my thoughts

While attempting to live my life without them

It's painful at times because I feel so alone

But I know they're with God

So, I strive to go on

Ma

I wasn't able to say goodbye or hold your hands and comfort you

As you slowly began to fade away into the afterlife

I wish I could've been given one last opportunity

To tell you I love you, Ma

And to hear you tell me you love me as well

Ma, when I received the news that you left me behind

I felt as if my heart had been broken into tiny molecules

And tossed somewhere far away in a galaxy of outer space

I miss you so much, Ma, that words can't begin to describe how I'm feeling

Losing you hurts me in ways I can't begin to explain

I'm so devastated, and I can't even fully grieve in peace

But regardless of wherever you are, my love for you will never decrease

The only thing that's keeping me strong is knowing you're with the Lord

After loving you for 45 years, it's so hard to know you're actually gone

I can't summarize how I'm feeling – or what I'm going through

But what I can say is thank you – for every lesson you taught me

Because without your teachings, I wouldn't be half of the man I am today

You showed me so many things in your own little ways

I'll always hold you dearly – and although I know you're in Heaven

Rejoicing with God and his angels

I still feel your presence as if you're right here near me

I Miss You, Ma

Should I be saying thank you and praising God's holy name

Because you're no longer in pain

Am I wrong for wishing I could still hear you tell me you love me again

And look into your eyes and see your smile?

Ma, you always told me to do good

But sometimes our love was just misunderstood

The love we share is far from being superficial

Believe me when I tell you I truly do miss you

And I know one day in Heaven, I'll see you again

Just because you're gone, don't think I love you any less

I'll still love you the same, and our love goes deeper than just our flesh

The only difference is now I have love and pain

Mixed together like sunshine and raindrops that just won't stop

This is just one of my ways of saying I miss you, Ma

If Only I Were Able to Repay You

If only I were able to repay you

For all that you've done

First, I'd start by saying, Ma

Thank you for raising me

And also for taking care of my daughters and sons

And for every gift

You placed it under the Christmas tree

And every birthday you celebrated

On behalf of me, my daughters and sons

You know, Ma, there's no way I could ever repay you

For all the sacrifices you made

Just know that I'm thankful and wish there was a way

I could let you hear these words I never got the chance to say

You even rewarded me when I didn't do good in school

Instead of doing my homework or participating in class

I was too busy trying to be cool

Now I realize I played the role of a fool

For way too long

And Ma, I'd like to apologize

For the way I carried on

Knowing I was wrong

I Wish You Were Still Here

Ma, I love you, and I wish you were still here

You taught me how to live and love

And how to conquer all my fears

When I needed someone to talk to

You were always there to listen

If I told you I was deeply troubled

You would always pay attention

No matter how many times

I'd run into your arms and cry as a little boy

You'd find solutions to my problems and fill my heart with joy

I Know You're with God

Ma, if you can hear me

And I know you can

Watch over my children

Help them to understand

Teach them Heavenly ways

So they can make it to the pearly white gates

I know someday in due time

I will see your face

I love you so much, and I know

I never got a chance to tell you goodbye

But I know you're with God

Watching over me from the Heavenly skies

There Are So Many Things I Miss About You

There are so many things I miss about you

And it's not just your cooking

Raised on an island, born in Brooklyn Kings County Hospital

You were the role model everyone wanted to follow

And be just like

You were the thread that kept the whole family tight

Whether near or far, I'll love you for life

And you will always be my hero whether you're alive or gone

Ma, my love is everlasting, just like yours

When others needed help, they'd eagerly knock on our door

And ask to speak with you

Because you'd do the things other people wouldn't do

You'd give your shirt off your back

If someone else needed you to

Ma, I saw the side of you that was always willing to help

You'd care for others so much more than your own self

I know God is so happy to have you in His upper room

And in His presence

You always loved the Lord, so keep preaching His message of hope

To all the lost souls in this universe that sometimes feel alone

I Live Better Today

Although I constantly slept around and clearly upset you

When I needed a lawyer, you came to my rescue

You'd give me your last if that's all you had

And even though you think I'm crazy

I love and respect you for that

You used to tell me to stop smoking weed

But I never would listen

If only I would've stopped smoking

And started paying attention

Then I wouldn't have to pay these prices I'm paying

Or be in this position, if you know what I'm saying

But that was then, and this is now

I refuse to let anyone or anything slow me down

I learnt from my past, and I live better today

And I know in the future, I'll be A O.K.

Ma ♥ Bro

Ma,

Even though you're not here to give me advice

Or tell me how much you love me

I still act as if you're here

Because I know that's what you would want

I miss you, Ma

Thank you

Even though I can't hear you tell me

Don't do this or *don't do that*

Now I understand why you always tried to guide me

In the right direction

And always had my back

Bro,

You were like the big brother I never had

I could always go to you for advice

There were times I wanted to lose it

But you pulled me back and gave me instruction

I miss you, Bro

Thank you

If Mommy could see how much wisdom you gave me

She'd be so proud of you

I know that both of you are looking down from Heaven

Proud of the man I've become

And bro, even though you were younger than me

You acted so much older

These are just some of the words

I wish I would've told you

Something I Feel You Need to Know

This is something I feel you need to know

Every day I wake up, I wish I could tell you I miss you, bro

If only I could breathe the breath of life back into your lungs

And hear your humor as jokes roll off your tongue

Punchline after punchline, that's how you delivered your jokes

You weren't selective with catering to all types of different folks

You made everyone believe you had an arsenal at your disposal and a bag of tricks of ammunition

You could captivate crowds and cause everyone to listen

When it came to dismantling your competition, nobody knew what to expect next

I watched you tell jokes that sometimes caused others to get vexed

And you knew just how to diffuse a situation once it started to escalate

I didn't just lose a brother, I lost a best friend the day you departed

So take this as my dedication

Bro

I didn't have the chance to tell you goodbye

I'm stuck here hurting, but I know you're with God

I wish I could've told you how much you meant to me before you departed

But I'm pretty sure you know that is not the way I wanted

And it's not what I wished

You had a heart made of gold, so you'll always be missed

Just thinking about you now is bringing tears to my eyes

King Sol, I miss you so much

You were always so wise

I remember all the times I came to you for advice or to get a laugh

Just knowing you're not here

Makes me so sad

My Mentor

You're my mentor, and you taught me how to rap

When you would spit your flows, you were always laid back

As I listened, I could imagine you blacking on a track

Your flow was incredible, and you're so unforgettable

I still remember the rhymes you used to utter

Because your metaphors were smoother than butter

You had your own style that I especially like

You didn't even need a crowd

Yet you still ripped the mic

If it weren't for you and your flow being fluid

I don't think I would've been

Too concerned with listening to music

You were the first emcee that made me pay attention

To the raps lyricists uttered

And still to this day

I look at you as if you were my big brother

You Held Me Down

You held me down when I needed you most

I will never forget all that you've done

No questions asked, you did it all out of love

I hear you now and know that I'm blessed

Through blood, pain, tears, tribulation and stress

You stuck by my side when all Hell broke loose

So there's no reason for me to second-guess

Because I know you're the truth

My brother, my brother, in you I confide

Whether times were good or bad, you've stayed by my side

And that is a debt I can never repay

When I couldn't see the light, you showed me the way

My brother in Christ, you know who you are

Keep your head up and shine like a star

I Know You Love My Brother

I know you love my brother, and I love you for that

You still go to his gravesite, and it makes you feel sad

Your heart is filled with love for my brother

That's what makes you do the things you do

I used to look into my brother's eyes and could tell he loved you too

He used to try to hide the way he truly felt

But I know that look of love because I once had it myself

It was like staring in a mirror at my own reflection

As I watched him smile

And if there's one thing I know, it's that you made him proud

Don't question his love because he's in Heaven, still gazing down

To wherever you are

Because a blind man could see

The place you hold in his heart

Pop Pop ♥ Nana

You were like a father to me

You taught me how to do chores

And take care of the people you love

When I was young

I wanted to be just like you

Pop Pop, you were true

You loved Nana all the way to her last breath

Nana died a sudden death

I still don't know the cause

As I watched her in the casket for the last time

I felt overtaken with grief and disbelief

Pop Pop, you were a man of peace

As far as I can remember

And I know you'll always love my Nana forever

Nana

You opened up your doors when we had nowhere else to go

You made me bring wood into the house whenever it snowed

You told me to feed the dogs and give them water each day

You made me keep my elbows off the table

And say grace before I ate

You'd take me with you when you used to drive the bus

You taught me the difference between my needs and my wants

You'd sometimes discipline me, and I thought you were being too tough

But what I didn't realize then

It was all for my own good

If I could breathe the breath of life into your lungs

Nana, I surely would

God bless you, Nana

I wish you nothing but good

The Good Old Days

You let us stay at your house

When we had nowhere else to go

I remember them days like it was yesterday

Walking to Four Brothers or the Chinese store

To buy boxes of Little Debbie cakes or pork fried rice and chicken wings

Me and my brother

Old timers giving us dollars off the street

That was the good old days

Now everything's changed

I remember your favorite show on TV was *Lifetime*

You loved to watch the episodes over and over

Daytime, nighttime, it didn't even matter

While the birds chirped

Cat roamed, and dogs laid down in the hallway

Or in your bedroom

I remember you always saying, "Get 'em Babe!" to Kojack

What happened to the good old days?

You Taught Me How to Play Chess

You taught me how to play chess and think outside the box

You loved drinking Wild Irish Rose; that's what I remember about you, Pops

I think about you from time to time and wonder how you're doing

You had good and bad ways, but everyone does; that's part of being human

You taught me when to throw a punch and how to use my feet

My mom said a good run is better than a bad stand

Because sometimes you gotta know when to retreat

I paid attention when she used to speak

I close my eyes and visualize the two of you

Sometimes, as I sleep

You never encouraged me to be the average person

Selling drugs on the street

I remember you had a head full of curly gray hair

And a mouth full of missing teeth

6 Feet and 7 Inches Tall

A gentle giant, that's what you were

You stood 6 feet and 7 inches tall

At your wake, they said you didn't care for basketball

Who would've thought? I guess not me

But not everybody cares about sports, My Great Uncle Rodney

My grandmother's brother

You used to tell me to be careful on my dirt bike

Those were the good old days

Thinking back to my past life

I miss you, Uncle Rodney

But I know you're in Heaven with the Lord

Watching over the rest of the family

How does it feel to have a new set of eyes?

You survived on Earth 24 years blind

You're a survivor; that's just the way you're designed

Spread your wings and fly

And tell Big Momma, Josephine and Skilly I said hi

You're Not My Pops

You're not my pops, but you helped raise my sons and daughters

You're not my pops, but you chose to marry my mother

You're not my pops, but you treated me like your son

You're not my pops, but you loved my family as one

You're not my pops, but you still stick around and help with the bills

You're not my pops, but I love you nevertheless

And just having someone like you in my life

Makes me feel like and know I've been blessed

Daddy's Little Girl

When I had you, I was happy and sad

Because I knew as soon as I saw your beautiful face

Someone was going to try to treat you bad

When I had you, I wanted to have a boy

But instead, I got a girl

I should have taken that as a signal to slow down

But I was too busy speeding

Every day I woke up, I was risking my freedom

Taking chances to support you and put clothes on your back

I had all kinds of hustles, from gambling to selling crack

Because for Daddy's Little Girl, I'd do whatever it took

I'm so sorry I broke your heart

I should've never chosen to live life like a crook

I Hope You Can Forgive Me

I never really had the opportunity to get to know you

But I love you, nonetheless

You'll always be a part of me

My precious bone and flesh

The sun chose to rise on you on the 20th of October

I would've stayed in the hospital the day you were born

But I couldn't because I wasn't sober

That's one of many regrets I live with

In many ways, I guess you could say

I deprived myself of mental nutrition each and every day

Having to deal with the reality

Of having two newborns blew me away

I hope you can forgive me for the pain I caused you

I don't know what else to say

But I will always be there for you

Josh

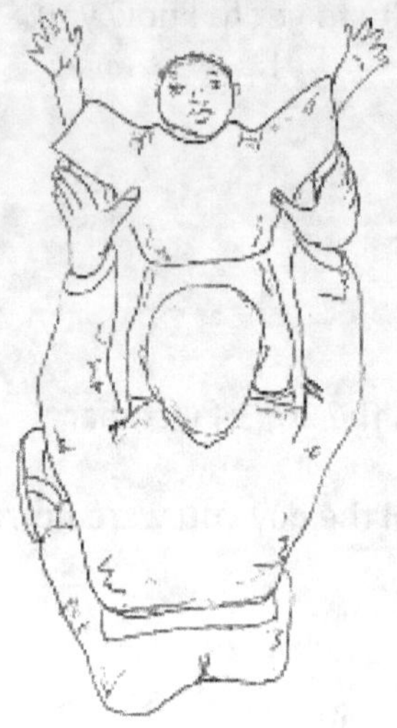

You remind me of myself in so many ways

I know your life has been tough, but in due time, things'll definitely change

It's just a phase you're going through

I've been there before; I'm just an older version of you

Keep reaching for the stars, and eventually, your dreams'll come true

I love you with all my heart

My young little lad

Although our ages may be different

You're quite like your Dad

I hope you always know how precious you truly are

Even though I haven't been there physically

I'll always love you, Josh

Sam, Live Your Life Like a Turtle

Sam, you want to choose your own path and make your own decisions

I just constantly pray you don't end up in someone's psych center or prison

In so many ways, you make me remember the things I was doing

When I was your age

I wish you'd take off the rollerblades that I know you can't fit

You want to be grown so bad, but you should enjoy being a kid

You're my junior, and I love you to death

However, sometimes I feel as if I'm wasting my breath

I try to guide you as best as I can

Yet you're so determined to be your own man

I can't hold your hand and help you make it over your hurdles

But I wish you'd slow down and live your life like a turtle

If I Had a Son That I Never Got to Raise

If I had a son that I never got to raise

What would I say?

I love you, and I'm sorry I wasn't truthful sooner

But if my future is brighter, yours will be too

All my life, there were things I could do

But I wasn't confident enough to take the risk

Now I realize I'll do anything for my kids

I've always been filled with love

That's just who I am

And if you're out there, my son, I hope you could understand

I love my children, and I pray they love me

If I had a son that I didn't know

I wouldn't want him to be anything like the past me

I'd want him to be responsible, strong, and a leader

But most of all, I want him to be a believer

In Christ and God, first and foremost

Then, I'd want him to believe in himself

And if I didn't know him

I would hope that he could forgive me

For not being a better father

And letting my circumstances trick me

Granddad so Proud

Wow, you have the most beautiful smile

Wow, you make me, your granddad so proud

I can only imagine how pleasant you are

You shine as bright as an Eastern star

Every time we talk, you're always so witty

And as far as beauty goes, God blessed you with plenty

I love you, my little love bug

And I wish you nothing but the best

Just know when you get older, life's surely going to put you to the test

I hope you pass with flying colors and end up successful, nonetheless

I Watch in Admiration

He fights life bravely, although many call him crazy

His name I won't mention because I'd rather not be offensive

Yet, I'll give a brief description of the person I see

He's a tall African American standing about 6'2" or 6'3"

He is unable to walk on his own, although he constantly tries

I watch in admiration as he pushes his wheelchair with pride

While battling cancer and being practically blind

This man I speak of is a true friend of mine

I offer him advice when I feel he needs help

But sometimes, he tells me to keep to myself

I Know How It Feels

Listen to me when I say

I was once in your shoes

I understand exactly what you're going through

I know how it feels to be disabled

But God gave me the will to get my circumstances back

And for that, I'm forever grateful

Once upon a time, many years ago

I traveled along the same path you're on

Where I felt like, *What else could go wrong?*

When I couldn't walk and fell down

Sometimes, others would laugh at me like I was a clown

Which made me angry, frustrated and annoyed

But regardless of what they said

I knew I couldn't let my confidence become destroyed

So I held my head high

Until I was able to fly

Because I knew God would help me

And He'll help you, too

All you have to do is try

Then watch what you can do

S.M.

I appreciate the visits on the weekends

And the telephone calls you accepted

I appreciate the advice you gave me when I needed support

I appreciate the help you offered me when I couldn't do it alone

I appreciate the food you brought up when you came to see me

I appreciate the times you came up to play chess

I appreciate the insight you offered on my work

I appreciate the way you motivated me

I appreciate you showing me which path I should take

Thanks, bro, and if you ever see me slipping

Don't want until it's too late 'cause I don't want to be in that position

Brothers

I have so many brothers

Though we all come from different mothers

One I was birthed with

Some I grew up with

Some I met in the streets

Some I formed alliances within prisons

Some I was introduced to in psych centers

But regardless of how many brothers I've had over the years

I love all my brothers equally

And that will never change

Because all my brothers are my brothers for life

We might not always see eye to eye

We might let each other down sometimes

We might not always be there when we need to be

But someday, things'll get better

I know they will

Your Love for Me

You left me for another man

Was that part of your plan?

Yet you still answer the phone whenever I call

When I ask for your help, you're quick to lend a hand

You raised a child of mine that didn't come from your womb

Anytime I need advice or help, you always came through

You're someone I can really talk to

About any and everything without being judged

Although you're just my friend now, you're someone I once loved

We share a bond that's impossible to let go of

Thank you for always showing me unconditional love

Your love has no end

Thank you for always being my friend

I Truly Am Grateful

It's friends like you that make the world incredible

You're someone to me that's so unforgettable

It's friends like you that make my life absolutely livable

You don't know the effect you have on me

But you push me to my peak

And as soon as I accomplish one of my goals

The next one I'm eager to defeat

Before I met you, all I had was a head full of dreams

Now, my life feels as if it's going upstream

And I just want to say thank you

Because if you haven't noticed

I truly am grateful

Thank You

Not only have you helped me find my way through the darkness

But I've also come to understand we do make great partners

There's so much I accomplished with the help of none other than you

In more ways than one, you made my hopes and dreams come true

And I just want to say thank you for everything you've done

Because even though we're only friends, I know you do it all out of love

Without you, I wouldn't be as successful as I am

And although our relationship is strictly platonic,

I'm quite certain you can understand exactly how I feel

Because you probably feel the same

You taught me lessons about life, and now I'm ready to change

Thank you

You Made Me Realize the Power Words Have

Thank you for being good to me

When other folks misunderstood me

You helped me open up those closed doors

And made sure I knew my worth

You also make me feel like I found my reason

For being here on Earth

I was sent here to sprinkle love on others

I want the best for all my sisters and brothers

Just because we weren't raised under the same roof

Don't mean jack diddly squat

Because God wants us all to flourish

But a lot of us act like we forgot

Let's come together and build an entirely new nation

For the lost and misled forthcoming generations

You made me realize the power that words have

With you by my side, I feel oh so glad

Thank you for being there

Just let me know if there's anything you need me to do

I wrote this poem for you

I already know I said thank you

But I just wanted to let you know

You have the qualities and characteristics of an angel

A Token of My Love

You always treated me equally

You were one of the first people that believed in me

We'd sit and chat so frequently

When I was lost, you drew a map for me to follow

You taught me a wise man's mind should never be shallow

You told me to be patient and wait for my tomorrow to come

I felt like my life was over when it hadn't even begun

You seasoned me like a chicken ready to be fried

When I felt so lifeless, almost ready to quit, you brought me back to life

You encouraged me to keep going when I had all that I could take

You accepted me for who I am

Even after I admitted that I made mistakes

When I told you I wasn't perfect

You weren't quick to judge

So, take this poem I wrote

As a token of my love

My red-haired friend, I remember you well

When I needed some guidance, it's like you walked me through Hell

You Inspire Me

With every step I take, you're right here by my side

It took me quite some time to find my peace of mind

Whenever I need guidance, you always offer advice

In humungous ways and minute ways, you've completely changed my life

I love you, my true friend, because I know that's what you are

It's everything about you that makes you shine just like the stars

I have never met anyone who loves the way you do

I used to think that most people had ulterior motives

But you changed my view

And now, I see life from a whole different perspective

You inspire me to want to take my life in a totally different direction

Indebted to You

I'm indebted to you for many reasons

You've been walking me through

What I should and shouldn't do

For several seasons

How do I repay you for all your kindness?

That's what I'd like to know

My only thought is by starting off

By saying *thank you* nice and slow

Without you, I wouldn't be where I am right now

Because it was you who helped me turn my world around

In a positive direction

When you entered my life

You entered my life like a hero in a movie

Or an angel sent from Heaven

Shine Like a Shooting Star

I can't thank you enough for everything you've done

And it's crazy because

You never cease to amaze me

You're always willing to help free of charge

You do have the biggest heart

You don't just think about yourself

You kind of remind me of myself and how I used to be

Back when I was able to lend a hand

When others acted like they couldn't understand someone in need

I was the friend they depended on for relief

Now it's like no one can understand my grief

But you

And honestly speaking, that statement has a lot of truth to it

As I glance down the corridors of my mind

I could see I'm starting to get used to it

You're unlike any friend I had in this world

You're like a mixture of Wonder Woman and Super Girl

I just can't believe how sincere you are

You don't even try and shine like a shooting star

We Can Change the Universe Together

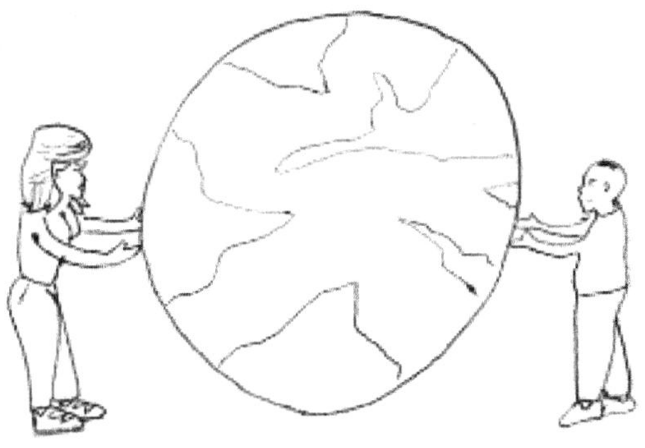

Someday, I hope I can repay you

Yet now all I'm able to say is thank you

To me, you'll always be amazing

You stuck by my side as I went through numerous changes

You don't know how grateful I truly am

For having someone so loving as my friend

You make me feel as if I could accomplish any one of my goals

You're someone who fills up my heart, mind, spirit and soul

I pray someday that we can change the universe together

You can use your influence and charm

I'll use my words

And someday, we'll make the universe better

Part III: Poems of the Heart: On Love and Lovers

My Story of Love

Sometimes, I just want to find someone to love

Sometimes, I think I have already found love

I came a long way from loving myself

I want to put someone first

But I don't know if I'll ever trust again

I tried to give my heart away so many times

But it just wouldn't love how I wanted it to

There's only been two different instances

When I can say I was totally in love

I loved other times, but not like when I was *in love*

Back then, I was so intoxicated it felt like I was on drugs

My first heartbreak hurt me so much

I couldn't respond to hearing the words, *It's over*

I just walked away feeling detached and sober

Not knowing what I wanted to do,

I felt so lost and blue

Then, the second time, I was in love

Distance and time tore my relationship apart

Not to mention

I didn't appreciate what I had when I had it

When I should have been playing my part

That's my story of love

And the two women that broke my heart

I Crave Love

Love is a two-way street

Some people search their whole lives but never find love

I wake up and think about love

I go to sleep thinking about love

I wish I had someone to love

But the truth is, I don't

I had love once upon a time

But I don't have love anymore

Like any other human being on Earth

I crave love

Yet, I'm a selective lover

I don't just give my heart away so easily

I have been hurt too many times in the past

And now I know the difference between

Being in love and loving someone

I experienced both

I crave love each and every day

Yet I'm not willing to give my heart away

But if love is meant for me

I guess it will find its way

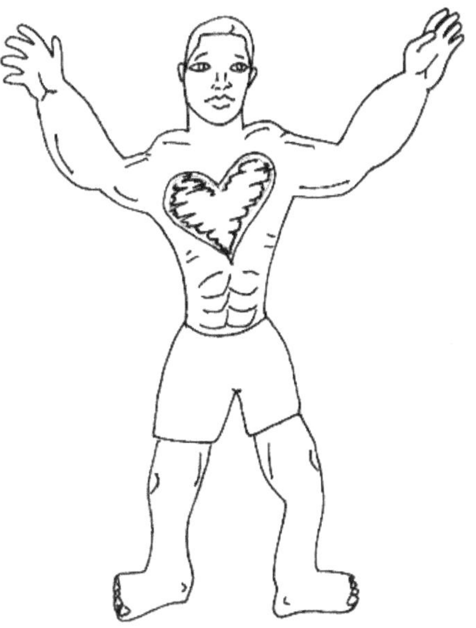

If I Ever Find Love Again

Love won't give up on you

And you can't give up on love

You gotta keep on searching until you find it

Once you find it, hold onto it

Like your very life depended on it

Or else you'll lose it

And regret it for the rest of your life

True love never dies

It lives on inside the heart, mind and soul of a person forever

I found true love twice

And I let it slip away from me

Because I couldn't see what I had until it was gone

Sometimes love'll blind you in ways you'll find impossible to ignore

It'll make you say things you don't mean

It'll make you do things you don't want to do

Because you want attention or want to know your worth

Love's crazy like that sometimes

It's unpredictable to a certain extent

All I know is if I ever find love again

I won't let it go

And I won't be afraid to commit

We Live, and We Learn

Sometimes, I feel like my heart is drowning

In an ocean full of tears

And all I can do is keep repressing my emotions

At times, it feels like love won't let me rest peacefully

And I can't help but wonder

Am I to blame for what I feel

Or am I taking responsibility for an emotion I can't control?

Either way, I look at it

It all boils down to the same conclusion:

Love is about taking chances

You never know who you're going to end up with

Or what will happen when the time comes

I loved, and I lost

That's just the way love goes sometimes

We live, and we learn

And we become better in time

Love Made Me

Love made me angry

Love made me sad

Love made me cry

Love made me mad

Love made me weak

Love made me stronger

Love made me restless

Love made me scream

Love made me feel like I was in a dream

Love made me joyful

Love made me calm

Love made me write some painful love songs

Everlasting Love

To find a love, a peace of mind,

A heart so pure, a love so blind

In the eyes of awe to seek and find

To plant a seed that sprouts and grows

A love so perfect that only one knows

To be so grand, can time withstand?

I dealt with many emotions

In my lifespan

Love

What exactly is this thing we call love all about?

Is love like a mustard seed when it's planted in fertile soil?

Or is it like the honor a mother feels when she holds her newborn baby in her arms for the first time in life?

Can love be compared to the most beautiful sunrise a person ever sets their eyes on?

What is love?

Is love the melody you hear in your ears as the birds chirp every morning amongst themselves?

Or is love the feeling you feel in your chest when you look into the eyes of your first love and realize the two of you were meant to be?

What Love is Like

Love can make you do things you never thought were possible

A little bit of love can go a long way

Could you imagine what the world would be like if love didn't exist?

Love can be expressed in so many forms

A mother's love is different from a friend's love

A child's love is different form a stranger's

Yet love is a necessity we all desire

Like oxygen to your lungs

And sugarcane or cotton candy on your tongue

When Love Strikes

When love strikes

There's no way that you can outrun it

Before you realize you have been hit

The blows just keep coming

It creeps so sudden

It's impossible to dodge

You could cover your head

But it'll swallow up your heart

You can't play your part

Once your emotions get involved

Because once they do

You'll turn into a whole 'nother you

Without the slightest clue

Of how the change took place

Another chapter in the book

Full of amazing grace

It's a beauty when it strikes

It's unlike the likes

Of anything you ever seen or dreamed

Or could imagine

Your heart'll beat with flaming passion

Your face'll get flushed

From the rush that you feel

And when you think you had enough

Love'll crush you still

My Love

My love is endless, and it can't be measured

When I decide to love, I love forever

My love is crazy, and it has a mind of its own

When I decide to love, I engrave my love in stone

My love is adventurous, and it's impossible to predict

When I decide to love, I can cure the brokenhearted and sick

My love is patient, and it takes its sweet little time

When I decide to love, I give my body, soul and mind

My love is everlasting, and it never goes away

When I decide to love, I show love every day

Falling in Love

Falling in love is like being on a roller coaster ride that you never want to end

It goes up, it goes down

And makes you scream from the top of your lungs, *I'm in love!*

It twists and turns and drops so unexpectedly

You can't predict what turn it'll take next

But you'll still want to ride to the very bitter end

It's scary sometimes

Then, other times, it's fulfilling in ways you can't begin to explain

Love'll make you feel alive, wanted, and appreciated like never before

Then, sometimes, love can make you cry tears of joy or agony

There's nothing worse than losing someone you love

I know because it happened to me

It'll make you think about all the things

You could've and should've said and done

While you had the opportunity to do so

But didn't

Falling in love can make you feel so alive it's like your soul's been set on fire

And every ounce of air you breathe belongs to your significant other

Falling in love is just a wonderful feeling two people share and experience with one another

Pleasure, Pain, and Mercy

Love is all about taking chances, and life is sorta the same way

When you find someone who makes you feel worthy

Make sure you tell them that every day

Don't be afraid to give your heart away

I know opening up is probably one of the hardest things to do

Because nobody wants to look like a fool

But if the love is true, it'll find you no matter where you are

You just have to be willing to reach for the stars

And let love take you on its romantic arms

Of pleasure, pain, and mercy

What Love Can Do

You see, you can never tell when love is going to strike

It'll creep into your life like a blind hit or a thief in the night

And you can't outrun it, so it makes no sense to try

Love has the power to make the strongest person swallow their pride

When you search for love, you may never find it

But when you least expect it

That's when the lovebug'll creep up on you

And leave you blinded

Love can be like a fairy tale or a dream come true

And for those of us who are superhumans, love is like kryptonite

We all know what it can do

It can make you feel weak in the knees

Or contaminate your mind, body, and soul like a disease without a cure

Love can be painful or quick on the draw

Love can build up an empire or destroy an entire nation

Love is patient, kind and amazing

Love is a blessing of the Lord's creation

But it's invisible to the naked eye

Sort of like a spy

Love is like a rainbow shining in our hearts, souls, and minds

Yet you can't see it, touch it or taste it because it's faceless

One thing I think we all could agree on,

Love is not basic

Love comes into our lives like an alien on a tiny little spaceship waiting to abduct us

Even when we don't want it to

Love can feel strange in our veins

And it also has the power to uplift us

Or cause us a tremendous amount of pain

In Order to Find Love Sometimes

Love'll pass you right on by if your eyes are closed

In order to find love, sometimes

You gotta be willing to get go of yourself completely

And turn into a whole new creation, even though it might not be easy

You gotta let your light shine

Like a celebration taking place within your heart, soul and mind

When a person finds love, you can see it written in their eyes

And all over their face

Because love'll make you feel like you're floating in outer space

Just to find your other half

The best love of all

Is the love that makes you laugh

And the love that lives in the present

Plans for the future

And learns from the past

And when the right time comes

Says, *I do*, once the question is asked

I Can't Wait

I can't wait to find the love of my life

I know she's out there somewhere waiting to be found

When I find the apple of my eye

That'll be the day I smile

I'm going to make sure she feels royal

She's going to be the one I spoil

I plan to treat her with the utmost respect

And every day, I'm going to tell her, *Sweetheart, you're the best*

I want our connection to be based on more than just flesh

I'd like to be the man of her dreams

And the only one capable of fulfilling her needs

What I Want

I want a girl, woman, lover and friend

I want to give my heart to someone who's loving never ends

I want to find someone that's always down for the ride

I want to build a relationship that can't be broken with time

I want to find someone who's always willing to chat

I want to find that special someone who'll always have my back

I Just Want Love

I just want to find love

I don't care what color she is

I don't care if she's from Europe, Africa, Asia, or Japan

Russian, Jamaica, France, or Thailand

I want to find somebody that makes me proud to say she's mine

I want to find somebody who's going to love me for life

And be there for me even in times of strife

I want to find a wife that I can build with

Someone who'll love me whether I'm penniless or a trillionaire

I want to find someone who'll always be there

To soothe, comfort and care for me

Who can make my life feel like I'm living in a fantasy

My Love Lasts for Infinity

My love lasts for infinity

It's not just here today and gone tomorrow

It lives on endlessly

I don't just give it away and take it back whenever I see fit

When I love, I love

To the fullest extent

And I love unconditionally

That's why I'm so hard to forget

I rely on the Lord

To give me my strength

To scale life's mountains

While searching for inner peace

A lot of my knowledge, wisdom and understanding

Came from being raised on vicious streets

Is It Me?

Is it me, or am I blind?

I'm searching for a love I just can't seem to find

If only I were able to open up my eyes

Then I'd see who has the potential to be my queen

It's as if all I do is daydream

About the woman that I have yet to see

I crave someone so pure to connect with me

That I can take as my bride

Because I want to feel appreciated

Deep down inside

I want to wear my heart on my sleeve

And that's how I feel

Though some might find it hard to believe

The First Time I Fell in Love

The first time I fell in love

It felt like my heart melted in my lover's hands

Let me correct that,

The first time I fell in love,

I felt nobody on Earth could understand

What I was feeling

Because what I was feeling was beyond belief

It felt like every inch of my mind, body, and soul was on fire

And my heart was snatched by a thief

I felt like I was in a euphoric state

That I didn't want to escape

I felt like I'd become one with my lover

And nothing or no one on Earth could separate the two of us

The first time I fell in love

I just wanted to let the whole world know I'm in love

And I wasn't afraid to say how I was feeling

I wanted to shout, *I'm in love!* from the rooftops

Or the top of the mountains

And let the world see for themselves

I'm in love

Hand and Glove

I feel like I've known you forever

And the craziest thing is I just met you

I'm trying not to think about you, but it's impossible for me to forget you

With a face and smile as beautiful as yours, who wouldn't be drawn

But I'm in love with another woman, so I feel like loving you is wrong

Yet I can't help myself because you're so so so magnetic

When we're together, it's like I feel an electrical connection

And our plugs are just filled with volts of love

I think you and I go together like a hand and glove

From the Second I Saw You

I had my eye on you from the second I saw you

I wanted you to be mine right then and there

I love your smile, I love your face, I love your hair

I even love the way you stared at me

Once upon a time

When I looked into your eyes

I told myself, *One day, she's going to be mine*

And eventually, that date and time came

You're my dream girl, and I say it without an ounce of shame

I love you so, and I want you to know

Every day, I can close my eyes

And listen to my heart as it sings a song for you

Knowing that you're the only girl

That made my every dream come true

When You Call

Whenever I hear your voice, I come running

You're so far, yet you seem so near

I feel like you're the potter, and my heart is the clay in your hands

When you come around, it's like magic in the air

And music to my ears

My adrenaline begins to rush

I feel flush

I can't even think straight

It's like I have a sweet tooth, and you're the cheesecake

I always want a little more of what you have to offer

And when I'm not with you, I feel like I'm being tortured

I find myself following you around like a little lost puppy

And I'll always love you whether you're chunky, skinny, fine, ugly, or fluffy

No Disrespect

You make me want to stop everything I'm doing

And come chase you

No disrespect, but I wish I could taste your juices

Right here and right now

I wish I could turn the lights out

And make you climb your own walls

I'd use my tongue to undress you

And then I'd bless you in ways

I can't even begin to explain

Then I'd engulf you in pleasure and pain from head to toe

And let you feel the gift God gave me

While it drives you crazy

Because I'm far from lazy

I'll let you ride my Mercedes Benz

Just promise not to tell none of your friends

Because I don't want no one getting involved

In what we've got going on

No disrespect, but once I get started

The only thing I keep doing is going strong

Sweeter Than a Piece of Fruit

What would I do to have a piece of you?

Baby, you're sweeter than a piece of fruit

Can I call you my mango?

I won't mind if you call me Mandingo

Or Mr. Handle My Business

I'll knock them doors down like I got gifts, and it's Christmas

You don't just turn heads, you stop hearts when you make an entrance

I know you're shy, but honestly, that doesn't make a difference

I feel like there's some parts of me that I ain't get to show you

But I'm tryin' to get my bag right before I approach you

You Make My Adrenaline Rush

You drive me crazy, Miss Daisy

Come back into my life because this is where you belong

Your love is what gives me the strength to carry on

You make my adrenaline rush

Like Barry Bonds and Sammy Sosa mixed in

Sweet little kitty cat, I know you got Trix

Just like the white bunny rabbit

I'm an addict for your kiss

I close my eyes and visualize

The two of us reuniting

Because we'll always be inseparable

Like thunder and lightning

I'm a Victim of Your Love

You take my breath away whenever I see you

I close my eyes and dream of being with you

I'm guilty as charged of attempting to pry my way inside your heart

You smite me with your charm and cause me to feel restless

As I gaze at your beauty, I find myself breathless

I look into your eyes and feel as if I'm touching your soul

You make me wish I could taste you and lose all control

If this is a battle, I feel like I'm losing this fight

Oh, who are you but someone so beautiful that prompts me to write

I'm a victim of your love

Every day and every night

My Heart is a Furnace, Your Love is My Fuel

I wouldn't tell you I love you if I didn't

And I have way too much respect for you to treat you like a chicken

However, you need to know your love is finger-licking good

If I had it my way, I'd give you all I could

The love we share is misunderstood, but I'll never let you go

Don't turn a blind eye and act like you don't already know

I could take your mind to heights its never seen

And show you things that you can only dream

I want you to love me for me, no strings attached

And I want to be the one that always has your back

It makes me feel proud to have someone like you

My heart is a furnace, and your love is my fuel

I Love Everything I See

I know you love me, and deep down inside

Honestly speaking, I love you too

Love, I'd sport you like a crown jewel

If you gave me the chance to

I think any man that overlooks you

Is a damn fool for letting you breeze

You've got the whole package, and I love everything I see

If you were a dog, I'd definitely want to be a flea

Or if you were mine, I'd treat you like the Queen you are

'Cause you shine brighter than the sun, moon, and stars

Love'll Make You Say Some Crazy Things

Love'll make you say some crazy things

I just want a woman willing to give me a ring

I just want a woman who's not going to cheat

I just want a woman who wants to be loved

I just want a woman who despises drugs

I just want a woman I can built a future with

I just want a woman who's ready to commit

I just want a woman who's always resilient

I just want a woman who's witty and brilliant

I just want a woman I can confide in

I just want a woman who isn't a liar

I just want a woman who sets me on fire

I just want a woman who isn't already taken

I just want a woman who'll make me scrambled eggs and bacon

I just want a woman to lift me up when I fall

I just want a woman who loves with every ounce of her all

I just want a woman whose love isn't rehearsed

I just want that woman that'll always put me first

You

When I need someone to talk to, you're always there

You don't need to say you love me because I know you care

It's the love I have for you that makes me persevere

I'm just trying to do my best to make you understand

You're an essential part of my life, like the air I breathe

You're my dream come to life and my fantasy

You're the woman on my mind before I go to sleep

If I could, I'd bless you with all the finer things

Someday, I hope to give you pearls, rubies and diamond rings

I'm Practically Speechless

I'm practically speechless when I'm in your presence

My heart beats out of my chest as I gaze into your eyes

It's like my mind races into outer space whenever we're together

When I'm down, I think about you and start to feel uplifted

You inspire me with your words of wisdom

I can feel your aura as you align within my system

Let me be your native king

If only I had diamond rings

I'd give you one for each day

As a token of my love

For the words I've yet to say

In hopes that the love that we share

Will never slip away

You Make Me Wish

You make me wish I could just get in a car

And drive wherever you are

You make me wish I could just pick up the phone

And tell you I'm sorry for not calling sooner

You make me wish I could

Hold you as tight as I can and never let you go

You make me wish I could

Give you all your heart's desires

You make me wish I could

Write you a love letter every single hour of every single day

You make me wish I could

Take you somewhere, bend on one knee and propose to you

You make me wish I could

Do things to you I've never done to another woman

Can We?

Can we honestly say what we found is love?

I know you love me, and I love you as well

When I gaze into your eyes

I feel like I'm under your spell

I think you're beautiful just the way you are

But I'm well aware you're cautious of your heart

It's probably been broken by men who didn't understand you

Or treat you well

If you ever allow me to love you

I promise I won't kiss and tell

However, I just want to be the one

Who makes you feel swell all the time

And if you ever need a massage

Just let me know, and I'll gladly oblige

Like a Rainbow

You're kinda like a rainbow

You only come around once in a blue

I don't know what it is about you

That makes me desire you the way that I do

But I just can't get you off my mind

When I look at you

You make me feel as high as the clouds

Though you rarely even smile at me

I'm engulfed in your aura

And you had this effect on me

Since the second that I saw you

My Love for You

My love for you

Is like a flower seed that won't stop growing

My love for you

Is like a beautiful smile that never fades away

My love for you

Is like a gentle breeze on a hot summer day

My love for you

Is like a mockingbird that won't stop whistling songs of joy

My love for you

Is like a mother's love for her only child

My love for you

Is like Cupid getting struck by his own arrow

My love for you

Is like closing my eyes and being kissed for the first time

My love for you

Is like being on trial and found guilty of a love crime

You're Such a Tease

You're such a tease, and you lead me on

The games you play are oh so wrong

Although I'm strong, you make me weak

I'm attracted to you like a dog in heat

I think of you before I sleep

My precious cuddly, loveable sheep

To be with you is all I desire

You ignite my heart and set my blood on fire

The passion I feel when I'm with you

I say to myself, *If only she knew*

The stars in the sky can't even compare

How amazing I feel

Whenever you're near

I share these feelings that are trapped deep within

But for now, I realize we can only be friends

Just When I Start Thinking She's into Me

Just when I start thinking she's into me

That's when she decides to tell me to wait

It's crazy because when I look into her eyes

I feel like what we found is fate

But what can I say to cause her to think differently?

She probably thinks I'm crazy

But I'm a hundred percent certain she's into me mentally

And I'm into her too

But I want more than that

And until I get what I want, I'm not falling back

Or calling it quits

I can't wait to feel her lips and taste her saliva

Afterwards, I'm gonna set her body on fire

And be the man that she desires in times of need

When she's ready to love, I'll be ready as well

Right now, I'm so lonely it feels like I'm walking through Hell

And it's sad because she looks into my eyes, and she can't even tell

I try to tell her how I feel

But I don't think she's paying me any attention

I long for the day when I could let her know

My true intentions

Friend, Lover and Bride

You take my breath away when you smile

You enchant me with your style

To win your heart, I'd walk a thousand miles

I try to remain cool, but it's hard when I'm with you

Because you make me want to drool every time I look in your eyes

Oh, how I yearn and wish you were mine

I'd suck on your toes and kiss your thighs

'Til your body became hotter than the sun in the sky

Someday, I hope you'll be my friend, lover and bride

But until then, I'm going to continue to take my time

Loving You and Treating You as My Friend

I'd like to get to know you in more ways than one

I don't know what it is about you, but you make me feel like

I'm falling in love

With your small little gestures and sly remarks

I can't help but feel your love as it creeps inside my heart

Every time I'm around you, I feel like I'm in a trance

You make me want to ask you, *Are you willing to take a chance*

And let me be your man?

But I doubt you'll agree, and I don't ask because I'm scared

So I'll just keep on loving you and treating you as my friend

When I Look into Your Eyes

When I look into your eyes, I see you actually have respect for me

Like a shooting star, you came into my life so unexpectedly

And blinded me with your light

You make my heart rejoice in ways that are far beyond delight

When I look into your eyes, I don't just see an ordinary human being, what I see is

You're sorta like Harriet Tubman, trying to help others find the keys to freedom

When I look in your eyes, I see someone whose beauty isn't just skin-deep

I see someone with a heart so huge you can make others' hearts skip beats

When I look in your eyes, I see someone admirable, considerate, compassionate, and loveable

When I look at you, I could name a hundred more reasons if I really wanted to

I don't know what to do or how to respond to your mystical charm

That you so effortlessly flaunt without even being aware of

But you're someone whose heart contains nothing but real love

When I look into your eyes, I see someone so genuine, trustworthy and unique

That all the words in my verbal lexicon couldn't define how sincere

I actually believe your words are whenever I hear you speak

When I look into your eyes, it feels like I can stare deep down into the

Depth of your soul and see you for who you truly are

And it amazes me to say I've finally found a friend on Earth

With a heart more precious than rubies, diamonds, and gold

When I look into your eyes, you make me feel as if there's nothing I can't do

Because you're always encouraging me to try and give the world my best

Even if I'm happy, sad, angry, hopeful, or depressed

These are just some words I had to get off my chest

And when I look into your eyes, it not only makes me want to tell you

You're the best, and I'm always going to show you love and the utmost respect

For Better or Worse

For better or worse, I'm never going to stop loving you

In sickness and in health, I'll be by your side regardless of what tomorrow brings

'Til death do us part, not even the Grim Reaper can break our bond

Loving you is like watching the most beautiful sunset one can fathom

Having a special place in your heart makes me feel as if I'm royalty

To be a part of your life completes me in ways you can't even begin to imagine

Our love isn't just deep, it's complex yet remarkably strange

Because even when we're apart, I feel as if I can feel your mind, body and soul

Pumping through my veins

The foundation of our love overwhelms my inner being like a river of life

You fill up each and every crevice inside of me as if you're my wife

Mentally, physically and emotionally, you sustain me

And give my life more purpose and meaning

Without you in my life, I feel as if I'm constantly bleeding

From my head all the way down to my toes

Because I can feel our relationship all the way down

Into the depths of my soul

I Want to Be

I don't just want to love you,

I want to comfort you

And put your heart and mind at ease

And if you ever get restless

I want to be the one you need

When you're searching for your soul mate

I want to be the one you find

And if you ever feel alone or down

I want to be the one you call

Because I look at life like this:

You're mine, and I'm yours

And for you, I'll put my whole life on pause

Yeah, I know I have some flaws

But I'm working on ways to get better

And I'm just hoping you'll bear with me

And stay by my side forever

Adam and Eve

You move me in so many ways

You motivate me to change my view on life

Adam was given Eve

So, Eve was really Adam's wife

I realize I don't want to be alone

I want someone by my side

Because every man and woman needs to have a home

Adam and Eve's home was in the Garden of Eden

My home is not only in Heaven

But also outside the gates of freedom

I see myself happily married

With a family to raise

But first, something's gotta change

Then, slowly my life'll start coming together

I realize now I'm the one who decides

Whether my life's going to take a turn for the worse

Or get better

Dilemma

Although we live in two different worlds

I find myself drawn to you in ways I cannot explain

When I hear you laugh, I think of Cupid holding a dart

You possess some sort of key that's slowly unlocking my heart

I want to run away from your charm

But you smite me with your love potion every time I try

Your mystique keeps knocking me off my feet

I'm falling, I'm falling, I'm falling for you

I can't even deny

I'm head over heels in love with you

You've set my soul on fire

Maybe I'm just daydreaming

Or better yet, maybe this is all just a delusion I'm experiencing

I'm trying to put the pieces of this puzzle together

But I can't...

I think I've got a dilemma

Where Are You?

You don't need to be in my presence

For me to express my innermost feelings

Without you, I feel incomplete and obsolete

My heart yearns for your loving

I feel as if I'm nothing without you

You fill my heart with warmth and joy

It's your absence that makes me crave you like sugarcane

Within, I silently whisper your name

But all I ever hear in return is my own echoing voice

And it's driving me insane

Where are you, my love?

Why do you cause me so much pain?

I'd Love You Wholeheartedly

I wouldn't rush into anything

I'd take my time, and I'd love you wholeheartedly

If you were mine

However, it's a challenge for me to express how I feel inside

Because Lord knows I have been down some tough roads in the past

I gave my heart away to women that weren't built to last

And I expected to be treated like a King

When I knew they had no intentions

Of giving me their heart or a ring

But now I think I have found my Queen

Now, I'm ready to change my ways

And be with you for the rest of my days

I Wonder How Life Would Be

I think about you every day and every night

I wonder how life would be if you were mine

I can only imagine how our future would be if you were with me

If I were with you, both of our lives would be new

The sun would shine, the air would be crisp, and the sky would be blue

I'd breathe with you and live for you

And take away any thoughts that make you feel miserable

I'd light your life up and fill you with hope

And repair any parts of you that need to be repaired

And if you ever needed a friend, I'd always be there

If You Let Me Inside Your Heart

If you let me inside your heart

That's where I'll always remain

Sometimes, we'll see eye to eye

Other times, I'll cause you some pain

I'll never proclaim to be perfect

Because I know that's one thing I'm not

When your burdens are too heavy to bear

That's when I'll always be there

To help you, however I can

No matter how many storms arrive

You'll always have me as your friend

And I'll always be by your side

I Know You've Been Hurt

Together, we can build an unbreakable bond

I can love you if you let me take away all your scars

I know you've been hurt; I can see it in your eyes

And it's hard for you to trust because guys tell you lies

But if you give me a chance

I'll show you it's all about us

If you let me in your heart

I'll let you in mine

And show my love just gets better with time

I want to get to know you, and you want the same

So let's stop playing these childish little games

I Can Never Repay You, Although I'm so Grateful

If only I were able to shower you with gifts

I'd send you my love and seal it with a kiss

Whenever I call, you always come running

You're as sweet as apple pie or chocolate cake in the oven

You've been by my side through my ups and downs

And I'm so grateful for the love that I've found

When others turnt their backs, you still chose to stay

They told you not to love me, but you loved me anyway

I can never repay you for all that you've done

You inspire my heart and fill me with love

I could never repay you, although I'm so grateful

I could never repay you, although I'm so grateful

And no matter where you are, you'll always be my angel

You're Sexy, Kind, Intelligent, Unique, and Sweet

I owe you so much for all you've done

You painted my heart with portraits of your love

If only I were able to explain how much you mean to me

Then you would acknowledge all the beautiful qualities I see in thee

You're sexy, kind, intelligent, unique, and sweet

And still, to this day, you can make my heart skip beats

I love you with all my heart, mind, body, and soul

You're the one friend I have that I never want to let go

You Always

You always inspire me to want to be better

You always said you'd love me forever

You always made me feel like what we have is real

You always treated me with your kindness and respect

You always told me you loved me to death

You always wanted me to treat you as best as I could

You always felt like our love was misunderstood

You always loved me as is

You always told me we fell in love when we were just kids

It's Everything About Her

She has expensive taste

And I barely have enough money to get by

However, in the past, when we were together

We had some really great times

I'll always love her even though she's not mine

The way she plays the cut

Her first name should be peroxide

She's always there for me when I need her

She's not just my friend, she's a true diva

I tell her I love her, and she continues to question me

It's everything about her

That's what constantly impresses me

Sometimes, she makes me wonder what's written in our destiny

Nevertheless, I hope she'll feel the same

This is no ordinary poem

It's based on my love and pain

I Still Feel Like That

There's a part of me that I wishes I could see you

Because our love is an essential portion of my life

I don't need to say it, but I really wish you were my wife

If only I held the key to your heart

Then I'd have the power to light up your world whenever it gets dark

I love everything about you, from the good, bad, to in between

You're not only the love of my life, you're also the girl of my dreams

I go to sleep and wish I could see your beautiful face

Even in your absence, you still possess the power to make my heart race

You're the only woman I ever said I want to marry when I get older

I still feel like that now that I'm a grown-up

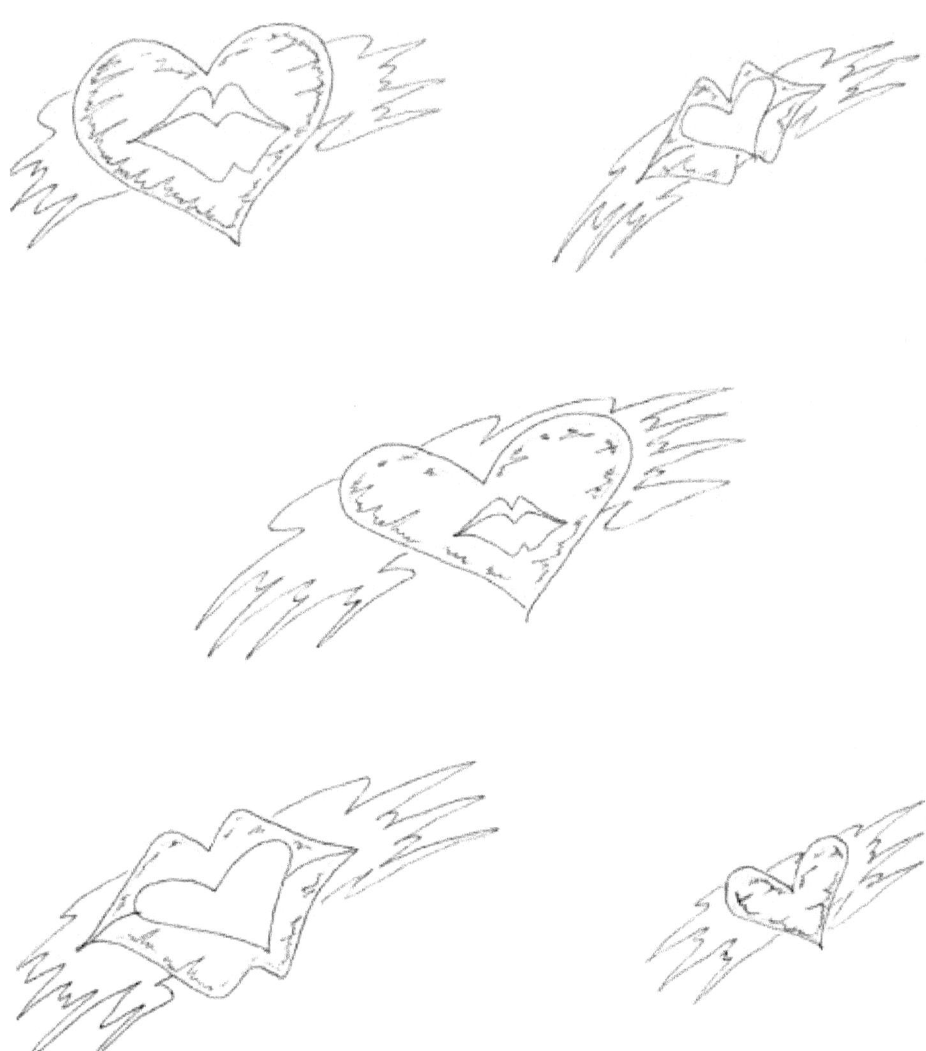

You're Afraid

I want to love you wholeheartedly, but you won't allow me to

You're afraid to give me a chance because you've been hurt in the past

I can understand how you feel; nevertheless, I love you still

I just pray someday your broken heart will heal

Loving you is the best thing that has ever happened to me

You make me love so naturally; I can never repay you

When I'm with you, all I ever want to do is say thank you

I can feel the magic in the air when I hear the sound of your voice

You always know the way to make my lonesome little heart rejoice

I just want to love you without being distracted by any disturbing thoughts

No matter where you are, my heart will always be yours

Love Me

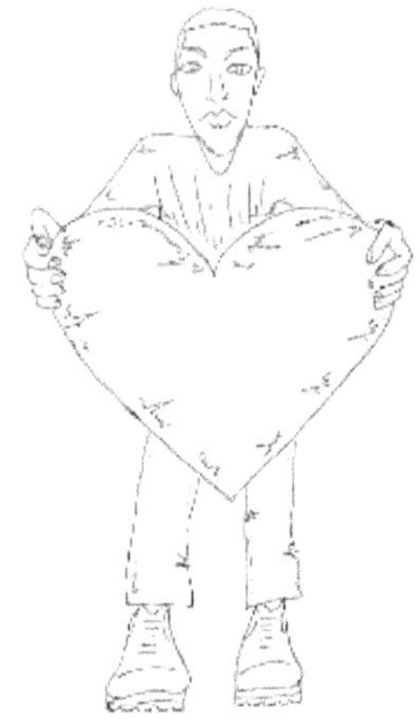

If I found a place in your heart

Please keep me there

I promise to love you regardless of what tomorrow brings

Through happiness, love me

Through the pain, love me

Through the hurt, love me

Through the transitions, love me

Through the ups and downs, love me

Through the grief and bitterness, love me

Through the loneliness, love me

Through the separation of distance and time, love me

Through the heavy burdens, love me

And likewise, I promise to love you in return

I Found a Reason to Love

I found a reason to love

When I look into your eyes

Although you're someone else's

I still wish you were mine

We live in two different worlds

Separated by distance and time

You send chills up my body

It's like you crawled up my spine

You're a beauty to behold

I'm so happy I'm not blind

If Only

If only you knew how long I've loved you

If only I could look you in your eyes and confess my love

If only we weren't separated by distance and time

If only I could take a photograph of my heart and send it to you

If only you were a mind reader and you could see how much I think of you

If only you and I could rekindle our flames of love

If only I could cause you to love again

If only I could make our hearts beat as one

If only I could open up your eyes and let you into my heart

If only I could plant a mustard seed of love inside your soul for me

Love and Deception

I burn and hunger – I hope and wonder

I constantly clutter – my mental with thoughts

Of you – my love so pure, of course

I've settled for less – and given my best

And what did you do – besides make me so blue

You tore out my heart – dismembered my flesh

You wore your disguise – and fooled me with lies

Unable to see – I was practically blind

I thought you were mine – my beautiful prize

Oh, what was I thinking – was I out of my mind?

Oh, how you had me fooled – I actually believed you were a crown jewel

My love, my love, my love – how could you be so cruel?

And treat me as if – I no longer exist

It doesn't make sense – why my heart still beats for you

A diamond in the rough is what I'll always see in you

Yet sometimes I feel like my reality is so unbelievable

As the Boat Sailed

As the boat sailed, we chatted and danced all night

The only thought on my mind was, *Hey, this girl seems so nice*

I asked you for your number, and you repeated it twice

That night, you approached me and asked what I was drinking

From the second you approached, I knew what you were thinking

And likewise, you could see my lustful eyes searching for freedom

As I gazed into your eyes

I looked past your disguise

And saw how badly you wanted some treatment

So, I gave you a chance to get what you wanted and needed

The next day, I called, and your mother answered the phone

And handed it to you

We had a brief conversation, and later on, you came through

Your cousins lived two blocks away from where I stayed

Shortly after that, you began riding my wave

You treated me good, so I opened up my heart

But when all Hell broke loose

That's when you left me to the sharks

So Long

The night I met you on the boat

You seemed so full of hope

I didn't know where our conversation would lead

But I decided I'd ask you for your number and see

If you were willing to give it

Being around you made me feel different

I remember so many things

Although you were only in my life for a minute

You used to make me feel like I was yours

At one point, you were someone I adored

In the end, turns out you loved others more

I can't blame you

And no, I don't hate you

I just wish we could try again

But I'm not gonna chase you

I already know I can't change you

The bond we shared, I didn't want it to end

You were my road dog

But for now, so long, my friend

I Truly Regret

I truly regret letting you leave without a fight

When I had you, I should've held on to you with all of my might

But I was young, dumb and sprung like the average teen

So I let you walk away when I knew I didn't really want to let you leave

Knowing my heart was broken and I could barely breathe

Because when I lost you, I not only lost my first love

I also lost the girl of my dreams

This Broken Heart

It really makes no sense to say how I feel

Because this broken heart of mine just won't heal

I try to force it to love

But it won't move on

I'd love to be in love once again

But every door I knock on, nobody's waiting to let me in

And I know in due time, things will feel differently

And it hurts because right now, it really feels like nobody misses me

But as soon as things start going well

That's when everything's going to change

And I'm going to be the one that's too busy to act the same

Or stop doing what I'm doing

Right now, my life feels like it's been ruined

But soon, things are going to start blooming and going extremely well

And then I'm going to feel like I never felt

Giving You Your Space

I can't quite figure out why you chose to hide your face

However, I continue to ponder these thoughts while giving you your space

I ask myself, if you wanted to be found, then why would you stay hidden?

Your love is the only key capable of letting my heart outside this prison

If I claimed I loved you any less, that would be a blatant lie

Nonetheless, sometimes, it still feels like I'm wasting my time

Words can't even express how I feel without you

Every day, all day, all I do is think about you

My heart is beating, but honestly, I don't want it to beat without you

I love you more with each day that passes

Your loving blows my mind away and turns my warm heart into ashes

I still feel fulfilled when I think about the bond we share

And even though I'm not looking you in the eyes, I still know you care

I Tried to Love

You hurt me, so I hurt you back

My heart was full of love until you turnt it black

I tried to love, but without you, it's impossible

I feel like my body's moving, but my heart's trapped inside a hospital

Sometimes, I close my eyes and dream I'm watching you

And it makes me feel cold and alone to know you have moved on

Yet my heart refuses to let go

'Cause these feelings I've got are too strong

So, all I do is continue to hold on

You Said You'd Always Love Me

The last time I saw you, you walked right by

As I approached, you waved goodbye

You stung me with your stinger with no remorse

Yet still, to this day, you dominate my thoughts

I miss you so much, sweet love of my life

Knowing you left me for some other guy

It hurts me to know you could do me like that

I can't figure out why

You said it was over and never came back

I ask myself why I am crazy for you

When you only express your love every once in a blue

You said you'd always love me

I just hope you still do

Instead of Searching for True Love

Instead of searching for true love

You'd rather just sleep around

I can't tell you how to live

But all them dogs gonna do is keep you down

While you're undressing for funds

The only thing them guys got on they minds is having a little fun

So go ahead, shake ya buns if that's what you want to do

Why do you always feel like you've got something to prove?

You're already one of the flyest females I've ever seen

You shouldn't need to degrade yourself in order to boost your self-esteem

What I Wanted to Do

I walked away, but it wasn't what I wanted to do

I only walked away because you wanted me to

I wanted to kiss you and comfort you when you told me it was over

But you looked like you had your mind made up

As you sat there on your sofa

I still remember how brokenhearted I felt that day

Hearing you say its over was like being kicked in my heart and slapped in the face

When you said those words to me, I was beyond sick

It felt like my world came crashing down, and I got hit with tons of bricks

I couldn't even fully respond because I was totally pissed

I walked away nevertheless

When I should've spoken and got what I had to say off my chest

But I left with a burning heart and scorching flesh

It Pains Me to Be So Blunt

As much as I want to believe she loves me

The truth is she probably doesn't

While I'm wondering where she is and how she's doing

She's probably taking care of her children and pleasing her husband

It pains me to be so blunt

But who am I fooling?

If she loved me, she would've never told me

To keep it moving

My Heart

Love, what's the sense of opening up my heart

Only to have it broken?

I feel like I've fallen so deep down

That my heart is no longer in motion

I would like my heart to burst into multiple flavors

As I express my thoughts and feelings on paper

But I have no one to share these feelings with

Yet somehow, my burning desires still exist

I've Hidden My Heart

I've hidden my heart

Because I'm tired of it being ripped apart by women

I probably would've given the world to

Had the world been mine to give

It's painful, because honestly

I'm not even certain how I should live

One minute, I feel like I'm on the hunt

The next, it's like I'm not even sure what I want

Do I want to be alone

Or would I be better off with a companion by my side?

That's one of the questions I ask myself almost every day

Because that's how I feel inside

I've hidden my heart

Because it's hard for me to give it away

And the saddest part about it is

I think about being in love every single day

Love Letters

You know all the right words to say to make my heart tick

But sometimes I feel it's all just a trick

You tell me you love me, and then you disappear

I pour my heart out and wish you could hear

Expressing my love is what I do well

But it's hard being strong while walking through Hell

I feel all alone with no one to love

And sometimes I question the man I've become

My heart's in your hands, so do as you will

I write you love letters but not for the thrill

And Since Then

She's searching for love she's unable to find

I call out her name with the voice of my mind

And proclaim my love, but she believes I'm a liar

Though she's the one who broke my heart and set it on fire

To this day, I can still feel the pain

Of being told what we had was over

'Cause that's the day I felt like Jackie Frost

Just woke up and decided to give me her cold shoulder

And since then, I haven't felt the same

And since then, I've been feeling bitterness and pain

I Feel So Betrayed

You don't just captivate me, you aggravate me at times

I feel so betrayed when you tell me your lies

About how much you love me and all

When some days, you don't even call

It's like sometimes I don't even exist to you

That's how it makes me feel when I don't hear from you

I wait for that phone to ring

But I guess you're too busy doing your own thing

And as far as your love is concerned

It's like I just can't get enough no matter how hard I try

I want to tell you goodbye

But it would hurt me even more

If I knew that I made you cry

Jezebel

If I'm a dog, and this world we're living in is crazy

Then life's a b-tch, and I ain't letting her birth my baby

Life and I have been through so much

I'm not even sure if she's the one I can trust

Because we both have issues that we barely even discuss

Every time I want to talk, she tells me to hush

And when I tell her I'm ready to settle down

She tells me there's no need to rush

And make hasty decisions

I feel like she's the warden

And my heart's locked up inside her prison

I still haven't learnt her real name

But she treats me like she's Jezebel

And I'm just another lame

Shattered My Heart

When you took your love away, it shattered my heart

Like frigid blistering winds, you tore me apart

Now, all I have to grasp are memories of you

I'm so sick inside, why'd you leave me so blue?

I don't know what to do, although I keep eagerly hoping

You'll come back into my life to repair this heart you've broken

Sincerely Yours

For what it's worth, I didn't mean to hurt you

I heard what you said, and honestly, I can't blame you

For thinking I played games with you

You know I'm always going to love you

Regardless of whether you love back,

I'm still going to love you, and that's a fact

I'm sorry for breaking your heart—it wasn't intentional

But you know something, you broke my heart too

I write about you because I still feel love for you

I'm not the type to give my heart away and take it back

Once I give it

I give it, and I just hope

It doesn't end up getting broken or cracked

I love you, and you know who you are

I don't need to say your name

Because you know who you are

I wish you were mine, but you're not

You're taken just like every other girl I loved

Sincerely yours

We Didn't Meet by Accident

We didn't meet by accident

It was fate that brought you my way

I didn't just start loving you, either

I've been in love with you

But how do you think it makes me feel to know you love someone else?

You know everybody's quick to judge me

But what would happen if you could read my mind or look into my heart

And see how deep my love is for you?

If you wanted to, you could find me, but you don't

If you wanted to, you could help me, but you choose not to

If you wanted to, you could love me unconditionally

But you decided not to

Yet I still pour my heart out to you

With the little love I have left

One day, you'll see that I'll always love you

We didn't meet by accident

It was meant for us to love one another

My Sweet Georgia Peach

If I could just look in your eyes

And say I'm sorry for all the wrong I've done

If I could just tell you, *Sweetheart, I wish we had a son*

If I could hold you in my arms

And feel your heartbeat against mine

Then I'd feel alive

Girl, you fill my heart with a fire I can't describe

I love you so much, and if I were able, I'd chase you down

To make you smile

My sweet Georgia Peach, you drive me wild

So Hasty

I should have learnt how not to be so hasty

And make rash decisions without thinking things through

When I found love for the second, third, and fourth time

I should have been true

But you know me, always moving at a fast pace

Thinking the world belonged to me

I guess that's what I get

For living inside a glass house and constantly tossing bricks

Now love's got me sick

And I can't find a cure

Of all the lovers that I had

None love me anymore

It's sad, but it's true

It's true, and it's sad

I brought this on myself

By treating the women I loved so bad

Oh, How I Wish

Oh, why can't I have what I want?

Why don't I want what I have?

Deep down, I feel so sad

I miss the love of my life, and I want her back

She's the one I want as a wife, that's a fact

I miss her and wish I didn't piss her off

Her skin was so soft, and her body was so right

Her face was so beautiful, and her mind was so ripe

Oh, how I wish she could hear me as I fiend for her

Oh, how I wish she'd return as I dream of her

She Said She Loved Me

She said she loved me

But she ain't really sure

Because if she loved me, she'd be knocking down the door

When I ask for help, she doesn't even reply

It hurts to know she can live without I

I miss her, so I'll always admit

She's the woman I'll never forget

When I think of her, I reminisce about our love

She came into my life like a blessing from up above

She Misses Me

It's as if I can feel her spirit reaching out to me

She misses me

It tears me apart to know I caused her silky heart to turn to stone

She misses me

Every day, I think of her and imagine how life would be if we were together—everything would be better

She misses me

I told her I would always love her forever, and I still do; my words are still true

She misses me

But she's tired of my lies and the games I play

But the love I have for her just won't fade

She misses me

She feels my pain

She misses me

And I think about my woman every single day

What I Miss

I find it hard to believe that you could just up and leave

Without saying goodbye

Even though I know we both told our fair share of lies

I guess back then just wasn't our time

You said you loved me, and I believed you

I said I loved you as well

Yet all we did was cause each other our fair share of Hell

I miss the way you smelled

I miss the touch of your skin

I miss listening to you tell me you love me

Over and over again

I miss you because I loved you

And you were my best friend

If Only I Could

If only I could hear you tell me you love me once again

If only I could hold you in my arms and feel the warmth of your body

If only I could write you a letter and tell you how much I miss and love you

If only I could see you smile that beautiful smile of yours

If only I could hear you tell me you love me still

If only I could listen to the sound of your laughter

If only I could make passionate love to you once again

If only I could tell you I'm sorry for breaking your heart

If only I could wipe away the tears I made you cry

If only I could listen to love songs with you like we used to

If only I could rewind time and tell you, *I love you, sweetheart*

If only I could find a place in your heart, mind, and soul

If only I could let you hear the poems and songs I've written for you

If only I could tell you how much I missed you all these years you've been gone

If only I could sweep you off your feet and make you fall in love with me

Beauty

Like a thief in the night

You came into my life and stole my heart

Then left me hanging out to dry

It hurts because you didn't even have the decency to tell me goodbye

I wonder how you're doing all the time

And if you are in the best of health

But sometimes I think the only person you care about is yourself

If only you would stop and patch up this broken heart that you helped ruin

Then that would probably make me feel a little less foolish

Sometimes I pick up my pen and don't know what I'm doing

And although I know you don't owe me an explanation

Sometimes, I wonder how I made it this long

Dealing with such a painful separation

Each and every day, you're constantly on my mind

Is it the power of your love that's been keeping me alive

There's not a day that goes by my heart doesn't long to be with you

You're the only woman that ever made me feel like my greatest dream came true

You're like a drug because all I do is fiend for you

Beauty is exactly what I saw then, and it's what I'll always see in you

Boom Boom Boom

Without you in my life, I feel powerless

And all I do is think of you

If only somehow I could rekindle our flame of love

And make those things go back to the way they were

Your absence still has me feeling numb

I feel like I've been run over by a car

And my heart's been shot by a gun

Boom, boom, boom

Yet all I do is think of you

I don't know what to do

Girl, you got me confused in the worst way

Boom, boom, boom

However, you're the only present I want for my birthday

I feel like we've known each other ever since first grade

Or maybe even longer

Boom, boom, boom

And the love that I have for you

Just keeps getting stronger

Don't Think I Don't Love You

Don't think I don't love you

Because the truth is I always will

I just need time to heal

You hurt my feelings for no reason at all

Then you're the first one to say you're keeping it tall

Yeah, if that's the truth, then tell me a lie

Because God knows there's so much I keep bottled inside

You take me for a ride and tell me you'll always love me

Then, as soon as I don't do what you want me to

You're so quick to judge me

I guess that's what I get for trying to give my heart away

I need someone who's gonna be there for more than just my darkest days

You discard me when it's convenient and blame it on me

Knowing damn well I gave you my love from my heart for free

I Hope That You and I Can Reunite

One day, I hope that you and I can reunite

I don't know how our one little argument turnt into a big ol' verbal fight

You told me it was over, and instantly broke my heart

I walked away that day feeling as if my chest had just been torn apart

You looked me in my eyes and ripped my heart to pieces

Back then, you made me feel amazing

Nowadays, you leave me feeling speechless

If only I could reach you and explain how I feel

Then I'm almost certain

Both our broken hearts would instantly heal

I Miss You So, My Angelica Star

I still think about you from time to time

There's not a day you're not on my mind

I wonder what you're doing and who you're with

There's so much more I miss than just your lips

Yet I'll always remember the first time we kissed

Your beauty to me is like a gentle breeze against my skin

I used to be so happy when you were my best friend

That smile of yours could always awaken my heart

I miss you so, my Angelica Star

I Never Had Another Lover Quite Like You

I never had another lover quite like you

Every day, you made me feel like the sky was blue

Being with you uplifted me in so many ways

I can't help but reflect back and wish our love would have never changed

If only I was bold enough to let you know what you meant to me back then

Instead of being long lost lovers, we'd probably still be best friends

Girl, I love you more than the air I breathe

And the raindrops that cover the Earth

And those are words you could most certainly believe

No matter who you're with, you'll always be my queen

I realize now I should have always put you first

I was only a teeny bopper until you introduced me to love

Before you came into my life

I had no clue what true love really was

Now I realize I made a grave mistake when I let you go

But you refused to budge and give me another chance

For what reason, only God and Heaven knows

I Missed You Then, I Miss You Now

Do you think about me still?

Does the thought of the two of us being together cross your mind?

The day I received your letter, I was so happy

Tears of joy came from my eyes

I thought that was the day you finally decided

To let me back into your life

I missed you then

And I miss you now

Because of the love I have for you

Will never go out of style

I miss hearing you laugh and making you smile

You were so wonderful to be around

I wish you'd come back

I miss you, my little dinky cat

The Most Sincere

I wish I were next to you

Holding you, kissing you, caressing you

I wish I could stare into those beautiful eyes of yours

And unlock your heart and your soul's doors

I miss you so, and I think of you every single day

You make me wish I would have never let our love fade away

I can't explain the stress, agony, and pain

That I feel knowing you're not near

Every day I wake up, I wish you'd reappear

Because to me, your love is still the most sincere

Beautiful Brown Eyes

I close my eyes and visualize

Your beautiful brown eyes

Gazing into mine

I can feel the warmth of your tender touch

Even when you're not present

Oh, how deeply I miss you

I yearn to kiss you

The taste of your tongue

Was like butter pecan ice cream

Melting inside my mouth

My precious Georgia peach

Just the thought of you makes me weak

If you were water

I'd crave a drink from your well

You used to enchant me and place me under your spell

Without you, I feel trapped

In a place between Heaven and Hell

When I Think of You

When I think of you, I remember how my life used to be

I remember our lengthy conversations that lasted through the night

I remember holding you and telling you how much I loved you

I remember how great your body felt against mine

I remember kissing your soft lips

I remember watching you smile

I remember making you laugh when I said something funny

I remember how amazing being around you made me feel

I remember hearing the sound of your angelic voice

I remember feeling like my dream came true

I remember loving you with all of my heart, body, mind and soul

More and More

You took my heart and breath away

From the first second that I laid eyes on you

You made me feel as if all my dreams had come true

I recognized your beauty

From the moment I looked into your eyes

I was head over heels in love, and it didn't come as a surprise

I loved you then, and I still love you now

You're the most beautiful woman I ever saw

And ever since you've been gone

The only thing I do is miss and think about you

More and more

Baby, Please

Baby, please don't say goodbye

When you feel like uttering these words

Just keep them inside

Show me that undying love that never tires

Even when I get on your nerves

Treat me as if we were truly meant to be

Because you know, like I know

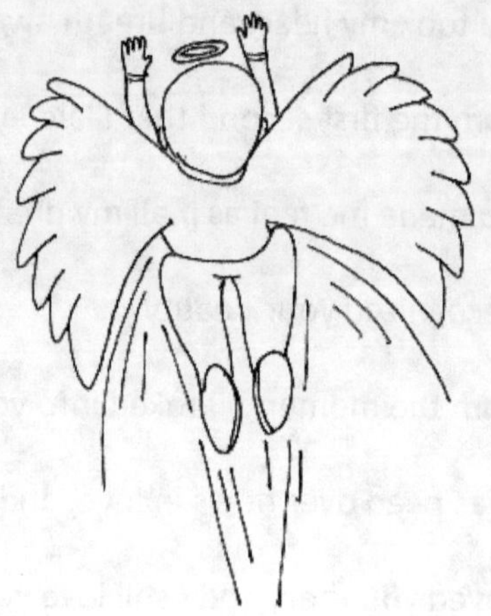

Our love is strong enough to calm the raging seas

It's always been like that

It's just for years, I've been putting up a front

It's your love that is lifting me up

I know I hurt you by violating your trust

But baby, please forgive me for all the problems

We've never discussed

Because without you by my side

It feels like my heart is being crushed

If Only I Were Able

If only I were able to hear your sweet voice

On the other end of the telephone

Then I'm almost quite certain I wouldn't feel so alone

If only I were able to wrap my arms around you

And hug you as tight as a polar bear

Then I know my cold heart would instantly warm up to your embrace

If only I were able to paint you a portrait

Of how my heart and my soul

Longs to be with you

Then you'd probably run back to me

And let me love you once again

If only I were able to let you see inside my mind

And stare at the foundation of my existence

Then you would understand

How lost and lonely I feel without you

And why I'm so persistent

Apple of My Eye

You'll always be the apple of my eye

I wish you would've never chosen to say goodbye

I guess what we shared

Wasn't as real as I thought it was

However, you were the first girl that taught me about love

If it wasn't for you

I probably wouldn't have a clue

How deep love can truly be

Before I met you, my heart was afraid to love

Until you came and set it free

Someday, You'll See the Light

If I could stop thinking about you, I would

But I can't, so I'm forced to write

I just hope and pray someday you'll see the light

Beneath the façade

Lays a man who has been hurt numerous times

I probably would still love you even if it was a crime

I'd still take the risk and see where it goes

Because no one knows what the future holds

Some find heartaches, some find rainbows

If you look deep within the windows of my soul

My pain will truly show

And you'll see how much you mean to me

I'm just a peasant searching for a queen

I don't have much to offer

Besides a warm heart, a diamond ring, bended knee

And vows I plan to keep

And I also think you're the woman

That can make me feel complete

Two Lonely Souls

Sometimes, I look at you and wonder:

Are we inseparable like lightning and thunder

Or are we just two lonely souls

Searching for our higher calling

And purpose in life?

You're seeking a husband who'll be true

While I'm seeking a wife who won't leave me feeling blue

I wish I could tell you how I feel

If only you knew without you

It's like my heart just won't heal

Silently and patiently

I count the days that you'll arrive

And tell me yourself

Your love has always been mine

And mine has always been yours

Whether together

Or separated by fences, states, or concrete walls

You'll always be the woman I adore

Ms. Universe:
You're the Missing Piece to My Universe

Ms. Universe

Why do you continue to hide your fire?

You tell me to be patient and wait

Knowing I love you more than anything in this world

It's hard for me because I dread the thought of losing you

You know how much I love you

But you refuse to accept me as I am

Without you, I'm lost

My heart roams aimlessly

To hear your voice would make me so weak

And fill me with superhuman strength at the same time

All I want to do is love you

And be the man you always wanted me to be

I need you to come back to me

Our hearts were made to love one another

You're the missing piece to my universe, Ms. Universe

I Want You to Know I'll Never Let Go

I want you to know I'll never let go

This place you have in my heart is yours and yours alone

I've held onto you for seven whole years

When my pain was unbearable, you wiped away my tears

I called out to you, and in return, you replied

I patiently wait for the day you'll be mine

Through the toils and snares and trials I must face

I eagerly hope to put smiles on your face

If I broke your heart, please forgive me for my deed

Because all I ever wanted was to be loved by a queen

Woman of my dreams, you know who you are

Come back into my life and mend my broken heart

You're the Sand, I'm the Sea

My life has no meaning without you

You make all of my dreams come true

When I think about you

I find myself filled with the greatest joy

One can ever imagine

The passion I feel for you

Floods every crevice of my entire being

I love you in ways words can never express

You are all I've ever wanted and needed in a woman

Your love has the strongest effect on me

I desire you in ways beyond belief

I feel like you're the sand

And I'm the sea

Or you're the prized possession

And I'm the thief

I want to steal your heart and make it mine

But as the saying goes,

Sometimes, love is blind

I Love You

Does she love me still – or am I just fooling myself?

I gave her my heart – I hope I didn't make a fool of myself

I told her I loved her then – and I still mean it now

Oh, how I miss her lovely face – and beautiful smile

Her love held me up – she was my crutch, the love I longed to embrace

When she came into my life – she made me feel as if I had more than enough

Before her, I didn't have the slightest clue – as to what true love really was

Yet somehow – I still managed to screw everything up

I was broken inside – until the second I met her

I glanced into her eyes – and my life changed forever

She put me back together – and asked for nothing in return

I told her I'll always love you – and I meant each and every word

If Only You Were Near Me

I can't stop thinking about you

I can't stop loving you

I can't stop missing you; without you, I'm miserable

I can't stop wondering how you're doing

I can't stop reminiscing about our past together

I can't stop hoping you'll come back to me and stay forever

I can't stop remembering how great it felt whenever we'd kiss

I can't stop thinking about all those little things about you that I miss

I can't stop wishing if only you were near me

I'd lick you up and down and treat you like cotton candy

Know Your Value

Where is the heart that compliments mine?

Where is my lover of quality time?

Where is my friend in whom I confide?

Where is the woman that's always on my mind?

Where is the soulmate whom I trust?

Where is the one woman I yearn to touch?

Where are you, my love? O, where are you?

Where are you, my love, O, woman, so true?

If only I could draw you back into my life like a picture

Or mold you like a piece of clay

Not only would you know your value

But you'd also give me the time of day

I'll Keep On

I'll keep on loving you even when it hurts

I keep putting you first even though it hurts

I keep on telling myself, *One day she'll be mine*

But who am I lying to?

You could care less whether I'm hurting inside

All you seem to care about is your image

And I'm someone who could damage your image

So I'll let you go free

Even though I want to hold onto you forever

I'll say goodbye

Even though it pains my heart to do so

But I'll still keep on loving you from a distance

And in time, hopefully, my broken heart can heal

And we'll both look at things differently

She Swept Me Off My Feet

My heart moved to her beat

She swept me off my feet

As if she were a dustpan sweeping up dust

She opened up her heart and immediately earned my trust

She's beautiful and full of charisma

But if you push her, she can be as cold as the winter's wind

I love her now, and I'll always love her until the very bitter end

She's my friend, lover and confidant

I trust with my life

I pray someday she'll settle down and become my wife

She brings me joy and makes me smile

She fulfills me in so many ways and makes me proud

I want to love her more, but sometimes, I feel like I'm not allowed

Drawn Like a Moth to Your Flames of Love

Can you hear my heart as it calls out to you

Or do I need to repeat myself?

Sometimes, I feel as if all I do is mistreat myself

I call out your name in vain

And all it does is cause me more pain

Which slowly drives me insane

Every time I try to walk away, I'm drawn like a moth to your flames of love

Your eyes used to tell tales as I gaze into your soul

You opened up your heart to me once upon a time

I hunger and thirst to know you as I once knew you in the past

I dream of holding and caressing you in my arms

Oh, how I long to touch you

I anxiously wait for your embrace

As I continue to make mistakes

And battle my own demons within

I sometimes feel as if I'm just never gonna win

The one heart I'm unable to obtain

I never thought one woman could cause me so much pain

Another Painless Poem

You inspire a fire filled with nitrous

That keeps spreading like a virus unlike any other likeness

As I glance within your scorned heart

That was once torn apart

I can feel the warmth of your energy

Like you're right here standing next to me

As you slowly begin to connect with me

In ways only God can explain

I silently shout

Oh, how I wish I could take away your anguish and doubts

Make your hurt my own

And turn your past, present, and future

Into another painless poem

Innermost Thoughts

I thought I was giving all of myself, but am I really?

As I jot my innermost thoughts, I wish you could hear me

I wonder, *Can you feel me like I can feel your presence in all I do?*

Once upon a time, you were my dream come true

But ever since you've been gone, all I do is hold on

To these memories, thoughts, and emotions of you

That somehow keeps me going regardless of what I may experience

One of my biggest regrets in life

Is not taking what we had more serious

And making a commitment when I had the opportunity to do so

Now I realize you had much more than just a heart made of pure gold

As I gazed into your eyes once upon a time

It was like I was staring at a butterfly

And I didn't just see pure beauty

I saw the most beautiful woman in the world standing in front of me

And as far as I'm concerned

That's the only woman you'll ever be

My Love, My Love, My Love

I love you, I love you, I love you

Even at the times that I don't want to

I miss you, I miss you, I miss you

You don't know what I would give up just to be with you

I reminisce, I reminisce, I reminisce

I still remember how magical it felt when we first kissed

Be mine, be mine, be mine

I promise I'll continue to love you for the rest of my life

My love, my love, my love

You must be an angel sent from the Heavens above

I need you, I need you, I need you

If you come back into my life, I promise I'll never deceive you

Send Me Someone

Heavenly Father, look down from your Heavenly sanctuary

And hear my petition

I'm lonely, send me a companion

I've traveled down this lonesome road for over 13 years

I need to be loved by someone willing to give me their heart

I want to find my soulmate

So teach me how to love again

Open up the valves of my heart

So love can pump through my veins

Send me someone that'll love me for me

I'm tired of going through life without a helper

Send me someone who'll be there physically and emotionally

I want someone to pray with

Send me someone who will love me

And who's also patient

The Things I Need

I need someone in my life that's going to treat me right

I need a friend first, a lover second, then a wife

I want to keep everything in that order

Once I establish myself

Then I want more sons and daughters

Because I want children to be named after my brother and mother, that are gone

So their names will continue to live on

I need a group of friends that'll offer advice

When I'm lost and can't find my way

And people that will help me live better each and every single day

A Woman

I love a woman who takes care of her child or children

I love someone who's not afraid to express how she's feeling

I love to be around someone that can make me laugh when I'm down

I love a woman who won't try to treat me like I'm a clown

I love a woman who focuses on the present

Prepares for the future and analyzes the past

I love a woman who doesn't always do whatever I ask

I love a woman who's always willing to volunteer some sexual healing and quality time

I love a woman who won't just "yes" me to death

I love a woman who listens when I talk

So I don't feel like I'm wasting my breath

I love a woman who's confident, mature and headstrong

I love a woman who doesn't just make tiresome speeches

But practices what she preaches

PART IV: PRAYERS AND POEMS TO OUR LORD AND SAVIOR

There are No Words to Summarize

There are no words that can summarize my love for You

My love for You has no beginning or end

I can't begin to describe the honor I feel

Knowing You love me as much as You do

You opened the doors of Heaven up to me

In ways beyond definition or explanation

My heart rejoices because of You

Thank you, Heavenly Father

One Day, I Hope to Hear Your Voice

One day, I hope to hearYyour voice

That is the only way my life will ever have true meaning

Your righteous hand guides those whom You choose to their destination

One day, I hope to be chosen by You, Almighty God

I've sought You all my life

My soul longs to know You in ways beyond expression

If only I were chosen to be Yours

Then, I would know the difference between

What's right and what's wrong

I wouldn't have to make my own decisions

And use my own understanding

Because You'd be my leader, teacher, and confidant

Precious Lord, I confide in You within my mind, body, and soul

Your love lifts me up in ways I cannot define

All my life, I wanted to be special in Your eyes

I wanted and needed You to take me as Your own

And teach me like You taught Jesus

I rejoice in the thought of knowing that You don't judge

Like humans based on mere appearance

You search the heart, mind, and soul of those in whom You find no fault

I wish I were faultless in Your eyes

So many times, I tried to help others

And upset You in the process

All I've done is search for righteousness

Yet all I've found was misery

I hope to one day be judged fairly in Your eyes

This world has broken me down in ways beyond belief

Every day, I cry out to You

With hope that I'm being heard

Dear Heavenly Father, I know that Your word is superb

I Find Fulfillment in Your Teachings

I look to You, precious Lord

For insight and knowledge of all things

Your ways are above the Heavens and Earth

You direct the paths of the righteous

There is nothing ever concealed or hidden

That You don't have knowledge of

How mighty and awesome is Your Strength

I wish I were like You in every aspect, in degree

For Your strength knows no limitation

How mighty and powerful are Your words

Which become flesh and give the hopeless hope

I've never known any being as powerful as You

All my days, I've searched deep within myself

For a part of me similar to You, my Lord

Yet, all my days, I've been lost

Struggling to find myself

And the true purpose of my life

As I ponder on Your ways

I find fulfillment in Your teachings

Unlock the parts of me that desire to be upright

Let my weaknesses be transformed and remade into a new creation

Take all my shortcomings and replace them with Your ways

Be my teacher, Lord God Almighty

Forever Your child,

Samuel

I Feel Like I'm All Alone, God

I feel like I'm all alone, God

Yet, I know inside my heart You're always watching

I try to be on my best behavior and make decisions

That I know You would approve of

But still, sometimes I fall short of Your Glory

Due to my own weaknesses

My life feels pointless at times

Then other times

I think there's more to my life than I realize

I read the Word and instill it inside my heart

And I find the strength to carry on

But then there are times when I feel weak and exhausted

I cry myself to sleep most nights

Pondering what I should have

And should not have done in the past

I have so many regrets that only You know

Not just regrets of the things I've done

But also of the things

I have seen done to others throughout my life

All my life, I wanted to help people

And I have helped people

But I haven't helped others the way

I wanted to help them

I wanted to be a person who one day

Changed the world for the better

I wanted to use the talents that You gave me

To help others out and make other people's lives

More meaningful and hopeful

However, all I think I've really done

Was make you more upset with me than anything

By interfering in the lives of others

I'm Searching

I'm searching for peace, enlightenment, and joy

Seeking God's face wholeheartedly

While trying to cope with frustration, oppression, and disparity

I'm bitter, yet I put on a smile

Like everything's okay

I hurt in a way beyond expression

I'm happy, but I'm sad

I was robbed by life

And beaten and battered at times

I've told lies to avoid

Telling the truth

I was once just an innocent boy

In the days of my youth

I planned on one day becoming someone great

But all I've really become is

Someone I hate

I tried to survive

At times, I swallowed my pride

Hoping to achieve my greatest goals in life

I wandered onto the most painful roads

I could ever stumble upon

My life is filled with so many skeletons

I wish I could just be reborn

And begin to live again

I was led astray and manipulated by sin

Although I try to elevate

I still don't see any good reason to celebrate

When all my hopes and dreams

Were destroyed as a young boy

I didn't have many toys

So I learnt to make my own

My father wasn't there to teach me

So I became grown

Before my time

I'd stare up into the sky

And tell myself that things will get better

With time

And God on my side

I Turn to You Always, Lord

I turn to You, Almighty Lord

For hope and strength

I open my mind, body, and soul up to You, Lord

My God, Your mercy endures forevermore

I am but a stranger wandering aimlessly without You

Guide me along Your path of righteousness

Take my hand and let my heart follow Your steps

Fill me with hope, courage, and prosperity

Make Your humble servant serve You and only You

Lead me along Your invisible road of redemption

Pierce my heart with Your arrows of holiness

Make my eyes ever seeing and all believing

Probe me inside and out

Flood me with Your compassion and mercy

Instruct me on the ways I should walk

Lift me up to new heights

Allow my weary mind to see things

From a holy perspective

Wipe away my tears

And fill me with Your wonder and awe

Take away my darkness

And fill me with Your forever shining light

Speak to me in ways like only You are able

Mold me into a new creation

Give me an understanding heart

And knowledge that surpasses the human mind

Smile down at me with Your holy blessings

Reach out Your mighty hand

And wipe away my sins of yesterday

Heal Me

I've fallen short of Your glory once again

How do I find the path of righteousness

While still unable to clear my conscience?

I ponder on Your words of wisdom daily

Let my cries shake the gates of Heaven

Hear my voice as I call out to You, O Lord

Fill me with Your wonder and awe

Be my shield

Give me the armor of righteousness to wear

Plant my feet on the ground, so solid that

I won't be shaken or uprooted by visible

Or invisible enemies

Let Your mighty towers of Heaven protect me against

The evil one who seeks to take my life

Let Your mighty powers cover the ground on which I stand

Guard me like You guard the gates of Heaven

Plant my feet so firmly that not even time itself

Will be able to erase my existence on this Earth

Heal me of my sinful nature

Cure me of my sicknesses

Let Your glorious light shine brightly

Within my soul

Transform me into a new creation

Toss my sins of yesterday into Your sea of forgetfulness

Help me, my Lord and Father

For I know Your mercy knows no limit

Teach me all of Your hidden mysteries

Remove the veils that block my inner vision

Let my deaf ears hear the sound of Your voice

As you call out to me, O Lord

Give me the strength I need to carry my cross

In the name of Christ Jesus

Hear me as I cry out to You, Mighty Lord

Forever Your son

I Searched High and Low

I searched high and low, Mighty Lord

To find your dwelling place of righteousness and holiness

I have never placed another God above Your holy name

You are the only God I've ever known

All my life, I asked You to teach and guide me

Yet all my life, I've been lost when I should have been found

I've always felt alone

So, I tried to make the best decisions I could

And stay on the path of righteousness

I'm 40 years old

And I'm tired of being lost

So I ask you, Lord, to strengthen, guide, and teach me

All I've learnt from others led me to become

The person I became

I'm tired of falling short of Your glory, God

I need You to come into my life and lead me

Because I can't do it alone

There is No Other God

I stare into the clear blue sky and wonder

Amazed by what You've created

Your power cannot be grasped

Your beauty has transformed the Earth

Into an amazing place

I think to myself, how magnificent are Your works of art to behold

Only You, God, could possess the knowledge of light and darkness

Of righteousness and glory

I serve a God who rises higher than the Heavens whose Word brings forth life

There is no other God besides You

God Almighty, I love You more than I love my own life

Yet I don't know how to fully serve You

I try to be as gracious as I can be with the grace you've given me

And even in my wisest ways, I cannot compare

To Your knowledge, wisdom and understanding

So I ask:

Teach me God

Show me the path of righteousness

Walk me towards the way of prosperity and holiness

Bless me with the riches beyond riches that I seek and desperately desire

Let Your light shine upon my face

Teach my mind how to be upright and forgiving

Let me learn to love those who persecute, mock, and stone me

Transform me into a new creation of light

Guide me when I become weak and weary

Pour Your spirit on me with Christlike love

Let Your ways become my ways

Fill me with a desire to serve You, and You alone

Whisper in my ears the ways in which

I should travel at all times

Psalm of Sam

I search for Your spiritual treasures, O Lord

I take pleasure in learning Your decrees

I write Your laws on the foundation of my heart

Stand by my side, O God of mystery and wonder

Don't let Your humble servant's pleas go unanswered

Come down from Your holy dwelling place

Save me and rescue me from all my invisible enemies

Who seek to devour my body like hungry lions

Transform the pits they've dug for me, O Mighty God

Into secret holy dwelling places of righteousness

Restore me as You would restore an innocent child

Take pity on me, O Mighty God

Hear my plea and toss my faults and mistakes

Into Your sea of forgetfulness

Let my transgressions be remembered

For they were mistakes

For You are a just God whose mercy knows no boundary

Let my voice open the gates of Heaven, O Lord

Hear my cry as You would hear the cry of a little child

Rescue me, Father, and bring me into the presence of

Your holy arms that reach out

And direct the paths of all those whom are lost

Be my comforter and redeemer

How Do I Serve a God So Great?

How do I serve a God so great?

Where can I find riches that aren't made by hands

To give to You for all You've given me?

God, I search my heart, mind, and soul

For a present to crown You with

Let my words be heard in the Heavens

God, without you, I'm nothing

I have no sense to rely upon

Because pleasing You is the only thing

That has ever truly mattered to me

I am nothing but a speck of dust

In Your universe of righteousness

God, All My Life

Like a lost sheep searching for its shepherd

I turn to You, O Mighty Lord

Be my protector

For who knows the paths of life

As well as the One who designed the paths?

Weigh my heart, O mighty Lord

Test my thoughts like only You are able

Remove my errors in thoughts

Judge me according to Your righteous scale

God, all my life, I searched for Thee

God, all my life, I pondered Your ways

God, all my life, I put my faith in You

Yet, all my days, I've been lost like a little child

Searching for Your Hidden Treasure

God, hear me now as I bring my supplications before You

Please hear me as I cry upon Your merciful ears

Which hear the cry of the persecuted and afflicted

Let my cry reach Your holy dwelling place

Grant my petition, O Lord, creator of the Heavens and Earth

Break loose the chains that bind me

Use Your wonder and awe to amaze all those who stand in my way

O Lord, they've dug pits for me, and they are eager

To devour me with their invisible snares

Let Your wrath come down and rain on my enemies

Hear my supplication and come to my aide, O Lord

My Children and God

I love all of you—everyone, just the same

Every single one of you bears my name

That's how much I love each of you

I don't have any favorites, no disrespect

But when it comes to love

The one I love the most

Is from up above

Hear the Desires of My Heart

O Lord, hear me now as I call out Your mighty name

Give attention to my prayers and hear the desire of my heart

Lord of Heaven and Earth, forgive me of my trespasses

Look into the core of my heart and see for Yourself

I did not intentionally sin against Thy holy name

Lord, my God, I was led astray like a lost sheep

Searching for a shepherd

I did not mean to arouse Your anger against me

I know the doors that are closed

Have remained closed because You have not willed them to open

I'm sorry, my Lord, that I have sinned against You

Please forgive me

I have been like a lost sheep

Wandering all my life

Searching for food, shelter, and clothing

Forgive me, my Lord

I was absentminded most of my days

I called out to Your loving name so many times

And did not know what else to do or where to turn

So, I tried to take care of myself however I could

I'm sorry for all my sins of omission and commission

Forgive me

O Lord, Hear Me

I bow down before You in submission

I surrender my spirit unto You

I call out Your name

O Lord, hear me

Be my guide through the unseen paths of life

Teach me Your wondrous ways

Let my mind be refined in Your sight

Set Your eyes upon every path I walk

Cast my iniquities from Your presence

Command my heart to obey the sound of Your voice

Let evilness flee from my presence

Take away the desire of my temptations to do evil

Grant my weary mind the peace I seek

To find You

Hide not Your face from my sights

Hear the petition of my heart

Just me accordingly

Probe me with Your rod of perfection

Screen me and make me whole in my mind, body, and spirit

Teach my soul to be obedient and submissive at all times

Direct my body to go before the paths of Your choosing

Cleanse my heart and take away my lustful vision

Make my paths completely straight in Your sight

Remove all my Earthly desires

Wash me and cleanse me

In the blood of Christ

I Anxiously Search

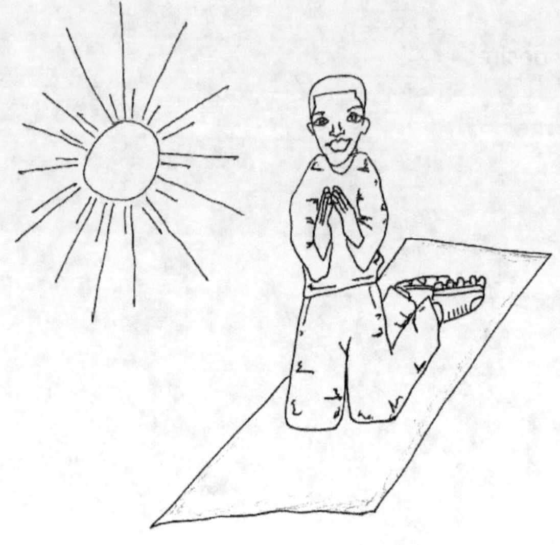

I anxiously search for Your hidden treasure

My heart belongs to You, O Lord, my God

I eagerly await Your arrival

Come into my life

Your kindness extends throughout the Earth and into the Heavens

There are none as great as You, Mighty Lord

Your powers are mysterious

You are a God of wonder

For no mortal possesses Your wisdom

Your ways are higher than the Heavens

I yearn to know You

I want to become like You

Take me and remake me

Teach me

Transform me

Into a new creation of light

Open my eyes to Your mysteries

Give me a new body

Teach me to be obedient and humble

Write Your laws upon my heart, mind and soul

Speak aloud to me

So my deaf ears can hear Your commands

Hear me as I pour out my heart to You

The Old Me and the New Me

I didn't choose to be the way I turned out

I tried to be as best as I could

But I kept falling short, a victim of circumstances

All I ever wanted was to be loved—and to love

But I didn't know how to give love

And I didn't know how to receive love

I was lost for years before I found Christ

But when I found Christ, my life changed

And the old me died

I became a new man—actually a child

Reborn in spirit, a renewal of my mind, body, and soul

Enlightened

And given a new life

Hear My Prayer as I Call Out unto You, Lord

Be my comforter, let your shimmering light shine upon my face in my times of despair

Hear my prayer, Lord, as I cry out to You on bended knees

Remove my flaws of character and fill me with a new disposition

Take away my loneliness and bless me with a companion that loves me like I love You

Send me an ounce of Your wisdom so that I'm able to discern

When I'm being led astray by outside forces

Draw me closer to Your invisible secret dwelling place

Shelter me in Your arms, O Lord of Heaven and Earth

Teach me how You taught Your prophets many years ago

Open up my heart and let me hear the sound of Your voice as You talk to me

Walk with me down the highways of life

Fill my heart with Your mercy, love, and compassion

Be a father to me, for I am fatherless

Guide me when I need guidance

Direct my steps when I see forks in the road

Cover me in the blood of Jesus

Anoint me with Your anointing oil of life

Prayer to God

I can't turn back; I've come too far

I worship and praise You, O Mighty God

Whenever I'm weak, You fill me with strength

Heavenly Father, it's You I beseech

To be in your presence is what I desire

You fill my heart with love and set my soul on fire

There's no other force that compels me like You

Heavenly Father, now I know Thou love art true

Please Forgive Me

Please forgive me for not speaking sooner

But if we don't come together, we might not have a future

In ancient times, Christ spoke about the end times being near

When natural disasters occur, and nation rises against nation

That's what I fear

Should I grab my torch and unleash massive thoughts

To these unfaithful nations that seem to be lost?

It's time for us to make a decision

And stay true and faithful to our spiritual religion

Let's try to be the servants the Lord and Christ envisioned us as

Now's the time for us to take off our masks

And let the world see us for who we truly are

Because we're all dream chasers, world changers, risk takers and shining stars

Please forgive me for not saying this sooner

But we need to come together so that we all may have a bright future

When I Look Up

When I look up in the sky at the sun, moon and stars

I can't help but acknowledge how beautiful Your works truly are

I'm amazed to be a part of Your wonderful creation, God

So, I say thank You for allowing me to be

Placed in a universe made so wondrously

By Your almighty hands

Because You possess the kind of love that never ends

You always win the hearts of the faithful, lonely, and lost

You also guide the steps of those You adore

Your love is stern yet never-ending

And Your wonderous ways are always trending

Call on the Creator

When all else fails, and there's nowhere to turn

Call on the Creator of the Heavens, Earth, and universe

In the Bible, scripture says faith is nothing without works

So let Your works be pleasing to the Almighty One

Who judges righteously and looks into the heart of mankind

Scripture also states that no man knows the mind or thoughts of God

For God's ways are not man's ways, nor are man's ways God's ways

God is an all-seeing, all-knowing, all-understanding God

When God looks at mankind and all His creation

God understands what man, woman, and child perceives

Even before we're able to grasp our own intentions or deeds

God is a God of love, always watching from the Heavens up above

Yet God is also a jealous God

Who hates when His servants serve two masters

God doesn't withhold His rod of correction when it needs to be drawn

And wherever God sends His blessings

That's exactly where they fall

I Plan to Be in the Presence of God Someday

I don't know what the future holds

But right now, I'm here on Earth

I plan to be in the presence of the Lord, my God, someday

When that day is, I haven't the slightest clue

I just hope God forgives me for not doing the things I should do

I don't call myself a Baptist, Protestant, or Christian

Yet I believe in the Holy Trinity

And I know I should be submissive

The Father, the Son, and the Holy Spirit motivate me

To want to be more than I already am

You see, I don't just want to be the average man

Who's in church wearing a flashy suit and nice shoes

I want to be a true child of God

Living, breathing, and relying on scripture

In times of victory as well as adversity

Just Like You

What makes me so different from everyone I see?

I call upon Your name from anywhere I may be

My faith keeps me whole, and it's all that I have

To walk in Your presence and cross all Your paths

You restore me with hope when I begin to feel drained

And I feel empowered as I call out Your name

O, Lord my God

Tell me, what shall I do

When the only thing I yearn for

Is to be just like You

O Lord of Heaven, let me lie on Your Back

So I can bear witness

And do as You ask

Father God, I Love You

Father God,

There's so much I have to say. I just don't know how to…

First, let me start by saying I'm sorry for all the wrong I've done. I wish I could undo all my wrongs and make everything right between us.

I love You so much, God. All my life, I've loved You and called out to You because I needed Your help and guidance. But all I've been is lost, waiting for Your response.

Believe me, I tried to be good and help whoever I could. It's just hard when every time I'm nice, I get repaid evil for good. That alone is enough to make a person lose focus. I know there are no excuses for all the wrongs I've done. All I can say is sorry and hope You forgive me.

But God, all my life, I called out to You and asked You to guide me, but I felt like You didn't hear me. I haven't once heard You reply, "I'll help," or even, "I'm listening." I just want to stop so I'll never ever commit another sin.

God, I love You more than I could ever say or fathom, and You know that I just need You to know how tired I am of being alone and lost. I have eyes, but they weren't able to understand and foresee all the trouble I found myself in beforehand.

God, I love You, but sometimes, I honestly think You're disappointed in me. I'm tired of being lost and blind. I want to be able to really see the light. I'm tired of lying and doing evil. I want You to guide me like You guided the Israelites and Hebrews.

Hear My Cry of Anguish

Hear my cry of anguish; be attentive to my petition of bitterness

Search my heart, mind and soul with Your righteous rod of perfection

Grant me the desires of my heart; deliver me from the snares nearby

Make me succumb to Your will, teach me, Lord, O, Magnificent God

Punish me for my faults, then let me flourish, Mighty Lord

O, Lord, I seek You with all my heart

As I've always sought Your presence

I know You're nearby, watching over me

Help me, Lord, Heal me, Lord

Transform me into a new creation of light

For with You, all things are possible, and without You, nothing would exist

Open my eyes like only You are able to

Take me as Your pupil and teach me Your ways of life

Remove all sinful ways from my being

Wash me in the blood of Jesus

Cleanse my soul in Your righteousness

Correct me of my faults and wrongdoings

Strengthen me with Your glorifying love of compassion and mercy

Look down from Heaven and hear my cry of despair

Hear My Petition and Prayer

I call out to You, O, Mighty Lord, in my distress

You are a God of mercy and forgiveness

O, Dear Lord, hear my petition and prayer

As my heart cries out to Your holy name

I need You, O, Great and Mighty God

For there is no God like You

You are the only God I've ever known

Praise be to Your name

God, lift me up high toward Your holy dwelling place

Refine me and speak to me in ways like only You are able

Hear my silent cry as I reach out to Your all-knowing ears of perfection

Judge me like You judged your prophets of old

Enrich my mind to the sound of Your voice

Guide my steps and teach me Your ways, Dear Lord

Be my redeemer and protector from the wicked one

Let Your light shine upon my face and throughout my mind, body, and soul

Forgive me for my transgressions

Bathe me in Your everlasting river of righteousness

Wash me in the blood of Jesus

Cast my sins into Your sea of forgetfulness

God, This is an Emergency

God, this is an emergency

I call on You, merciful Lord, to probe me thoroughly

And remove any and all things inside of me that aren't true and pure

Lord, loving, mighty, powerful God

I ask You to open up the doors of opportunity

So I can rebuild the communities

I helped destroy when I was unemployed

And I ask that You'll make it so I never relapse

And fill me with the strength to overcome all the obstacles I face

Because, Lord, I know I could do anything

With just a touch of Your grace

God, I'm Hurt

I'm sad, hurt, miserable, and lonely. I need your help.

You said, "Seek, and ye shall find." I've sought you all my life, yet all I've been is lost like a wandering sheep.

You said, "Ask, and it shall be given." I've been asking for You to help me all of my life, and I feel as if my pleas haven't been heard.

You've let me learn the ways of man when You could have taught me Yourself.

You said, "Knock and the door will be opened." I've been knocking at Your door all of my life.

Yet the door of happiness and peace has remained closed to me.

Come into my life and take away my pain.

And when I'm tempted to sin, teach me to refrain.

I Pray That You're Always Beside Me

I pray that You're always beside me

Your presence is all I need to guide me

I search high and low for Your righteousness

I strive to be like You in all I do

You rescue me from my troubles and give me strength in my times of need

Your fountain of life sustains my well-being

I yearn to know You, Dear Lord, and become like You in all I do

Your word inspires me to want more out of life

I find pleasure and delight in filling my heart with Your statutes

Oh, how I wish I could find Your holy dwelling place

To please You is my greatest goal

Strengthen me in all I do, Mighty Lord

Let Your light shine inside of my heart, mind, and soul

Overwhelm me with Your grace, mercy and compassion

Father me like You fathered Moses, Elijah, and Jesus

Take me and refine me like a loving father with a prodigal son

Mold me like a potter molds clay in his hands

Build me upon your mystery and wonder

Be my father, dear Lord, and teach me Your ways

I Call Upon Your Great Name

I call upon Your great name in my time of pain and affliction, precious Lord

How I wish to be heard by Your omnipotent ears

All my life, I've searched for You, Almighty Lord

I'm begging You to probe my heart, mind, and soul and see for Yourself

Whether I'd made the mistakes I made for my own selfish intentions

Or whether I was just trying to better my circumstances

And help others in their distress

I ask You to walk with me through these valleys I face

And be my guide when tribulation arises in my life

Teach Me My Faults

Father, what have I done to wrong You?

Teach me my faults so that I may please You

Open my eyes to Your all-knowing presence

Search my heart, test my thoughts, and remove my shortcomings

Let Your light shine in my eyes

Take away the darkness that clouds my vision

Take away the planks in my eye

Please hear me, Father, for You are the only Father I've ever known

Nurture my seed of faith so that I may blossom and become fruitful in all I do

And that I might serve You the way You desire to be served

Lord, I know with You, all things are possible

Fill my heart, mind and soul with Your ways and words of wisdom

Let me find comfort in Your word of truth and prosperity

Lord, hear me as I call out to You

Let the gates of Heaven open

Accept the sound of my repenting voice as an offering to You, Lord

I Will Always Praise You

No matter where I'm at, I will always praise Your holy name

O, Lord of Heaven and Earth, hear my petition as I cry out to You

I would like to be renewed in Your well of prosperity

Take my hand and walk me through the valleys of the shadow of death

Be my guiding light and mold me into a new being

Teach me Your righteous ways

Fill my heart with love, mercy, compassion and empathy

Let Your wisdom, knowledge and understanding overtake me

O, Lord, forgive me for all my wrongdoings

Place me on Your straight and narrow path

And give me strength not to wander off when temptation arises

What Would Happen If...

What would happen if all God was waiting for

Was for us to pray to Him and confess our sins?

What would happen if COVID was a plague from God

Put here on Earth to bring us closer to God?

What would happen if all we had to do was pick up our Bibles

And follow God's commandments every day of our lives?

What would happen if the only reason God hasn't spoken to us

In so many years is because of our own sinful nature?

What would happen if we all bowed our heads and got on our knees

And called out to God and asked for forgiveness?

What would happen if this generation were to call upon the Lord

More than any previous generation?

What would happen if God were right here on Earth in a human form

Watching everything that is going on, taking notes?

What do you think he would say about how the world is being torn apart

And how we're living each day?

Driven By Faith

I used to feel lost, and I didn't know which way I should turn

I felt as if I was living a life I didn't deserve

Yet somehow, I continued to smile in the face of adversity

Determined to overcome my trials and tribulations

As if they were nothing but a test from a prior enemy, I had already defeated

Suddenly, I looked the Devil in his eyes and shouted, *You've already been beaten!*

I refuse to let you or your demons stand in the way of me glorifying my Father!

Though trouble may knock at my door, and I don't know what to expect tomorrow,

I will humbly continue to praise my Father with every fiber of my being

Until my days on Earth end and my mission is completed

Thank You

Thank You for my mother and father, although they're gone

Thank You for my lovers, although they've abandoned me

Thank You for my children, although sometimes they don't always listen

Thank You for my friends who come and go as they please

Thank You for my lungs and the air that I breathe

Thank You for the gifts that You've given so freely

Thank You for blessing me with wisdom so others aren't able to mislead me

Thank You for granting me the strength to bear my burdens

Thank You for filling my heart with fire at times when I get nervous

Thank You for teaching me every lesson You taught me

Thank You for always having my back and being there to support me

Thank You for carrying me when I was unable to walk

Thank You for giving me a brain and teaching me how to talk

Thank You for changing me when I wasn't able to change myself

Thank You for standing firmly by my side when I felt like I had nobody else

Thank You for teaching me how to be humble, gracious and patient

Thank You for being omnipotent, forgiving as well as amazing

Prayer to God

I can't turn back; I've come too far

I worship and praise You, O Mighty God

Whenever I'm weak, you fill me with strength

My Heavenly Father, it's You I beseech

To be in your presence is what I desire

You fill my heart with love and set my soul on fire

There's no other force that compels me like You

My Heavenly Father, I know Thou love art true

Before I Found My Path

Don't be afraid to travel a different way

Because deep down, everyone craves change

Before I found my path, I was entangled in a zone

Now I know my way home

It's God that I desire

He's the only One I truly seek

He's my shepherd, and I'm His sheep

I love God with all my heart, mind, body, and soul

And wherever He leads me, I'll willingly go

Heavenly Father, Hear My Plea

Heavenly Father, hear my plea

Touch my life and set me free

Lift me up when I am weak

Let Your ways become my own

Enter my life

Lead me home

Teach me all Your glorious ways

Redirect me when I go astray

Lord of Heaven, hear my plea

When stress presents itself

Give me strength

When I speak Your name

Hear me and come quickly

Heavenly Father, always stay with me

And show me all the things

That I need to see

Open my eyes

To what You want me to be

Righteous Judge

Thank you for all you've given me

Without your blessings, I wouldn't have anything

You watch over me while I rest

Forgive me for all I confess

Strengthen me with all of my steps

Relieve me when I feel depressed

Lord of all, I know You're always nearby

Whether on Earth or watching from Heavenly skies

You hear the prayers of those You love

Creator of all and righteous judge

Teach Me

Walk with me down this narrow road

Be my guide, strengthen my soul

Keep me at peace when I begin to feel battered

Show me Your ways are all that truly matter

Hold my hand when I don't see straight

Remove my planks, unlock Your gates

Touch me in ways like only You're able

Teach me how to be humble and faithful

Take away all my lust

Let me become someone You can trust

Mold me like You molded Your Son

Forgive me for all the wrongdoings I've done

Touch me in ways like only You're able

In times of distress, teach me to be faithful

Teach Me Your Ways

Heavenly Father, Lord of all

Answer my prayers whenever I call

Love me, Lord, be my guide

Bring some peace to my weary mind

Love me like Jesus loved His disciples

Teach me how to live by faith and the scripture-filled Bible

Hear my petition as I call unto You

As valleys arise, walk me through

When I'm discouraged, keep me strong

Teach me Your ways, Almighty Lord

Lord

O, Lord, when I feel like quitting

I'm trying to remain strong

But the pain won't cease

Sometimes, I feel like

In order to deal with the pressure

I gotta turn into a beast

There's this voice inside I continue to hear

That tells me, *Keep pressing forward and have no fear*

So, instead of giving up, I continue to persevere

While searching for my true meaning in life

I realize I was placed on Earth

To praise You, Lord, and emulate Christ

Without You by My Side

We're all just searching for You in our own way

And we're trying to find You by any means possible

Some of us search with all our hearts

And some of us are just trying to find where You reside

Because we want to ask You

Why our life has been so combatable

It seems like no matter where we are

We're all just trying to find You, Lord

You're our Creator

You give our lives purpose and meaning

You make our hearts rejoice whenever You see fit

And for that, we love You, Lord

You've been with me down every road I've traveled

And I just want to say thank you

For bringing me the joy You brought me, Lord

I couldn't have made it this far

Without You by my side

And I also know that there is no secret on Earth

That I'm able to hide

I Take No Credit

I take no credit for this gift I've been given

I found myself in jails, prisons, and psychiatric centers

Who am I but a speck of dust

Or a grain of sand?

Yeah, I have gifts

But God is the One who has put these gifts inside my hands

I thank You, Creator, for all You've done

I also understand there's nothing new under the sun

Whatever has been done

Will be done again

I call on the Lord, my trusting friend

You hold my hand and keep me strong

And lift me up whenever I fall

I pray to You when I feel weak

The God I serve, it's You I seek

I Don't Know It All

I don't know it all, and you don't know it all

He doesn't know it all, and she doesn't know it all

We don't know it all, and they don't know it all

But you know who knows it all?

Jesus

He knows it all because He suffered more than any of us

He performed miracles and still got treated treacherous

He didn't even have a place to rest his head

Let alone a bed

In the end, they nailed Him to the cross

He suffered so our souls wouldn't be lost

Not only was He the sacrificial lamb,

Christ was bold enough to wear the crown of thorns

He died without breaking any laws and for a very good cause

He didn't repay good with evil like most people

Jesus is the man I wish I could be, and He has no equal

Thank you, my Lord, for being so good to me

How can a sinful man such as myself ever repay Thee?

I guess I'll start by first saying thank you

Whether on Earth or in Heaven, I'll continue to praise You

I'm Always Going to Believe in You

When I got in the car accident, I believed in You

When the doctor said I may never walk again, I believed in You

When I was in a wheelchair, I believed in You

When I had surgery after surgery, I believed in You

When I had a gun thrown to my head at fourteen, I believed in You

When I was being shot at point blank range, and a bullet went through my hoodie, I believed in You

When I was ready to jump off a bridge, I believed in You

When I got tazed all over my body, I believed in You

When they sent me upstate to defend myself, I believed in You

When I was in cars with people, and they got into accidents, I believed in You

When I got assaulted by the COs, I believed in You

When the police officers assaulted me, I believed in You

When my brother died, I believed in You

When my mother died, I believed in You

When my father died, I believed in You

When my grandparents died, I believed in You

When my Nana died, I believed in You

And know what?

Even when I die, I'll still believe in You

You're the Best

They tell me I'm lucky

Yet, I don't believe in luck

Good fortune comes from the hand, heart, mind and soul

Of the God in whom I put my trust

He walks me through valleys

And takes me to heights

That alone, I know I wouldn't be able to climb

But with my Lord

All things are possible

Because, unlike mortal men

His blessings are unstoppable

You can't block the blessings God is willing to give

If He's happy with you

He'll even find favor with your kids

From one generation to the next

I love you, Lord

Thank you. You're the best!

In addition to writing poetry, I have written many songs, including songs about God. I hope to publish a book of my lyrics one day, but I would like to share a few of my gospel songs here. I hope you enjoy them!

My Savior

This is my story – these are my poems

I call on my Savior – He keeps me strong

These are my stories – these are my psalms

I talk to my Savior – all day long

I am not perfect – sometimes, I'm wrong

But wit my Savior – life just goes on

I call on my Savior – And he picks up His phone

He says nobody's perfect – but life just goes on

This is my story – these are my poems

I call on my Savior – He keeps me strong

These are my stories – these are my psalms

I talk to my Savior – all day long

I am not perfect – sometimes, I'm wrong

But with my Savior – life just goes on

I call on my Savior – And he picks up His phone

He says nobody's perfect – but life just goes on

Verse 1:

I, lock and load – when traveling down these rocky roads

Hee he, hee he – ha, he ho

Now I'm 'bout ta do, everything – they thought, wuz impossible

When rating my lyrics – just say, I'm the most phenomenal

I wake up every day – and thank God for making it possible

'Cuz without Him in my life – none of my bars would be tropical

I praise Him for giving me the strength – to make it through all these obstacles

And also, for keeping my feet grounded – if u don't, see me scoring

That means – I'm playing D or rebounding

I don't have a college degrees – but I got street knowledge

The first dude, that slept on me – u might just read about him

My sixteens got, e'rybody – wanta, speak about 'em

I could turn a bad girl good – and cleanse the demons out of her

Or make a good girl turn bad – and bring the freak up out of her

Use ta, kiss and tell – but I learnt, it's betta ta keep it quiet

They probably gonna charge me wit arson – for setting these beats on fire

Push me in a corner – watch me turn inta, the equalizer

Punchline after punchline – now I got ya, speakers wired

As soon as I reach my peak – I climb even higher

My ultimate goal in life's – to find the road that leads to Zion

All this bickering – going on, and nobody speaks about it

I take my brain wherever I go – I never leave wit out it

<u>Chorus</u>:

This is my story – these are my poems

I call on my Savior – He keeps me strong

These are my stories – these are my psalms

I talk to my Savior – all day long

I am not perfect – sometimes, I'm wrong

But wit my Savior – life just goes on

I call on my Savior – And he picks up His phone

He says nobody's perfect – but life just goes on

This is my story – these are my poems

I call on my Savior – He keeps me strong

These are my stories – these are my psalms

I talk to my Savior – all day long

I am not perfect – sometimes, I'm wrong

But with my Savior – life just goes on

I call on my Savior – And he picks up His phone

He says nobody's perfect – but life just goes on

<u>Verse 2</u>:

I could really care less – what other people think about me

I keep it so funky – these bars just keep reeking out of me

I must be a problem – if I wuzn't, they wouldn't speak about me

Vicky, herself – couldn't even get a secret outta me

Started off in NY – and now I got a wave in Cali

I'm slick like B.I.G. – don't bring, ya babe around me

Lyrically, I'm hotter than flames – y'all heard about it in Maui

I work on my songs every day – like it's the grand finale

When I make my way to the top – trust me y'all gonna, hear about me

I ain't just start, turning up – I wuz, already rowdy

Just like that cat, Heathcliff – I'm searching every alley

Some dudes act like they want to smoke – then call the Federales

I already know the outcome – so I don't resort to violence

Sometimes, ya strongest words – are the ones u say in silence

I wuz, walking it out – when other dudes, wuz talking 'bout it

For years, I played games – and all I did wuz, waste my talents

I filled my heart wit, scriptures – and now, I'm breaking my silence

I had a slight dilemma – but finally found a way around it

No more government assistance – y'all can keep y'all public housing

My bars shine so bright – they got the stars in the sky astounded

When dudes wuz, getting Zzz's – I wuz, working on my albums

Every day, in the streets – I felt like I wuz hustling for outfits

Now I have exactly – what it takes to climb up these mountains

This is my story – these are my poems

I call on my Savior – He keeps me strong

These are my stories – these are my psalms

I talk to my Savior – all day long

I am not perfect – sometimes, I'm wrong

But wit my Savior – life just goes on

I call on my Savior – And he picks up His phone

He says nobody's perfect – but life just goes on

This is my story – these are my poems

I call on my Savior – He keeps me strong

These are my stories – these are my psalms

I talk to my Savior – all day long

I am not perfect – sometimes, I'm wrong

But with my Savior – life just goes on

I call on my Savior – And he picks up His phone

He says nobody's perfect – but life just goes on

You Can't Take

You can't take my joy

You can't take my joy

You can't take my joy away from me

You can't take my joy

You can't take my joy

You can't take my joy away from me

Everywhere I go – I'm taking my joy

And you can't take my joy away from me

Everywhere I go – I'm taking my joy

And you can't take my joy away from me

You can't take my joy

You can't take my joy

You can't take my joy away from me

You can't take my joy

You can't take my joy

You can't take my joy away from me

Everywhere I go – I'm taking my faith

And you can't take my faith away from me

Everywhere I go – I'm taking my faith

And you can't take my faith away from me

You can't take my faith

You can't take my faith

You can't take my faith away from me

You can't take my faith

You can't take my faith

You can't take my faith away from me

Everywhere I go – I'm taking God's grace

And you can't take God's grace away from me

Everywhere I go – I'm taking God's grace

And you can't take God's grace away from me

You can't take God's grace

You can't take God's grace

You can't take God's grace away from me

You can't take God's grace

You can't take God's grace

You can't take God's grace away from me

Heavenly Thoughts

<u>Chorus 1</u>:

Bless me with a solid heart – I'm tired of playing tug of war

Teach me how u taught King David – so I could luv u more

Bless me with a solid heart – I'm tired of playing tug of war

Teach me how u taught King David – so I could luv u more

Bless me with a solid heart – I'm tired of playing tug of war

Teach me how u taught King David – so I could luv u more

Bless me with a solid heart – I'm tired of playing tug of war

Teach me how u taught King David – so I could luv u more

<u>Verse 1</u>:

When I die – I hope I catch that flight to Heaven

Cuz I'm eagerly waiting – to reunite, wit all my brethren

It seems like I have been trynta find – the promised land, forever

It's hectic right now – yet somehow, I'm holding it together

I'm, sick – but slowly and surely, I'm getting better

Sometimes I wish I could pick up the pen – and write God a letter

If I could, I'd repent – for all the sins that I committed

'Cuz now, I'm older and mature – I'm starting to look at life different

No sense in beating around the bush – Lord, I know, I should've listened

Instead of becoming a criminal – I should've, turnt into a Christian

When u sent me those signs – that's when I should've paid attention

'Cuz, if I did – I would've never ended up in this position

I wuz a narcotic seller – and a marijuana abuser

Instead of chasing my dreams – I chose to live life like a loser

Just like the Ninja Turtles – I wuz raised in the sewers

At a very early age – I wuz playing wit Bazookas

I got my game from the addicts – hustlers, players, and the gangsters

When I turnt to the streets – I met some real risk takers

It seemed like, e'rybody – I knew wanta be famous

And all of their ways – ended up becoming even more contagious

Started off at the bottom – but I wuz always thinking of major

Just like the Koolaid Man – I always had that flavor

God, forgive me – for the things I did to get the paper

God, forgive me – for the things I did to get the paper

<u>Chorus 2</u>:

Bless me with a solid heart – I'm tired of playing tug of war

Teach me how u taught my ancestors – so I could luv u more

Bless me with a solid heart – I'm tired of playing tug of war

Teach me how u taught King David – so I could luv u more

Bless me with a solid heart – I'm tired of playing tug of war

Teach me how u taught your servant Job – so I could luv u more

Bless me wit a solid heart – I'm tired of playing tug of war

Teach me how u taught Jesus – so I could luv u more

<u>Verse 2</u>:

I'm supplicating right now – waiting for something amazing to happen

I'm seven thirty, Lord – please help me, get these stains out of my jacket

I'm tired of feeding into the fire – don't let these demons take me backwards

I got my knees on the floor – and my elbows on the mattress

Pops wuzn't present – so I grew up like a bastard

The evil one's real name – must be Satan the Assassin

But I refuse to let him or his henchmen – take my passion

I experienced more Hell – than the human mind can imagine

Lord know what prompts – my intentions, deeds, thoughts and reactions

U even know the answers – to all my questions before I ask 'em

Sorta like, Noah – my life wuz filled wit disasters

I wuz in Hell's Kitchen – flipping burgers wit no spatula

Knowing that one man – can never serve two masters

I could've gone to school – and become a preacher or a pastor

Instead, I chose the block – and lived the life of a trapstar

Lord, I ain't mean to be rebellious – but it came natural

Instead of chasing, righteousness – I chose to roam the streets

By the time I wuz, seventeen – I wuz already fighting police

I broke one officer's nose – because he assaulted me

I hate the way that it went down – but why lie on these beats?

I ended up with one and a half – to four and a half for doing me

They sent me upstate – cuz they ain't wanta see me free

I did, for three years – and got conditionally released

Before, then – they didn't wanta to open up the gates

Like Gretsky – I couldn't wait ta put back on my skates

I did my time, went home – and felt so outta place

Eleven months later – I caught a whole 'nother charge

Dudes jumped and robbed me – so I blazed the firearm

But I don't gotta tell u – cuz u know it all, Lord

They gave me seven years for that – and still, I remained strong

I ain't never been a bluffer – I keep my poker face on

If I defend myself – they are still gonna treat me like I'm wrong

And if I'm offending u, Lord – please forgive me for my song

Cuz, paradise – is the only place I feel like I belong

<u>Chorus 2</u>:

Bless me with a solid heart – I'm tired of playing tug of war

Teach me how u taught my ancestors – so I could luv u more

Bless me with a solid heart – I'm tired of playing tug of war

Teach me how u taught King David – so I could luv u more

Bless me with a solid heart – I'm tired of playing tug of war

Teach me how u taught your servant Job – so I could luv u more

Bless me wit a solid heart – I'm tired of playing tug of war

Teach me how u taught Jesus – so I could luv u more

Bless me with a solid heart – I'm tired of playing tug of war

Teach me how u taught my ancestors – so I could luv u more

Bless me with a solid heart – I'm tired of playing tug of war

Teach me how u taught King David – so I could luv u more

Bless me with a solid heart – I'm tired of playing tug of war

Teach me how u taught your servant Job – so I could luv u more

Bless me wit a solid heart – I'm tired of playing tug of war

Teach me how u taught Jesus – so I could luv u more

Part V:
Poems of Motivation and Inspiration for the Next Generation

Inhale, Exhale

When your problems feel like they're getting the best of you

And you don't know what else to do

Don't give up on yourself

Inhale, exhale

Take a deep breath when you feel overwhelmed by life and all its heartaches

Think about all the people who love you and how much you love them, and tell yourself,

I'll get through this. Even if it's not today or tomorrow, I will get through this one day. This is just a test. I'm experiencing stress.

Inhale, exhale

When it seems like there's no one around to hear you out or listen to what you have to say

And none of the advice others, such as friends and family, have offered seems to work for you no matter how much you apply it

Place your troubles in God's hands and trust in God.

Inhale, exhale

When someone says something so horrible to you that it makes you want to lash out,

Inhale, exhale and imagine yourself laying on a beach of any island of your choice

Listening to the waves crashing against the seashore

While being engulfed by 90 degree sun rays,

As the comfort of a crisp, cool, calm, gentle breeze brushes over your skin, tell yourself,

I'll make it through this like I've made it through everything else I've encountered in life.

Inhale, exhale

When your burdens become too big to carry on your own

And things don't go the way you expect them to:

Reach out to someone in your support network, such as family, friends, peers, associates or maybe even coworkers

And see what kind of suggestions or feedback they might have to offer

Incorporate their ideas or suggestions into your thought process

And use that information to make better choices and wiser decisions

Furthermore, when you feel yourself being triggered by what people may say or do or the events that take place in your life

Inhale, exhale

Then, use your consequential thinking skills

What I mean by that is weigh the pros and cons of the situation that's being placed in front of you

And think about what you have to gain from the situation

And what you have to lose

Then make the best decision you can make

Inhale, exhale

And utilize the coping skills you've learned over the years, such as watching TV, playing a video game or a card game, taking a walk, meditating

And do your best to deal with it

Inhale, exhale

Everything Changes

We're all born infants at one point in time or another

It makes no difference whether you're older than me or I'm younger than you

Our mindsets and characteristics began to transition as time went by

When we're infants, all we want to do

Is hold our bottles or teddy bears, suck our pacifiers

Cuddle in our favorite blankets or be held by our mothers or fathers

Or anyone else willing to show us genuine affection

It doesn't matter if they're our brother, sister, father, aunt, uncle, or so on

We just want to be cared for, like every other human being on Earth

And we want to be loved when we want to be loved

We're not concerned or prejudiced about where our loving's coming from

Just as long as we're receiving love from someone

When we're infants, we cry for different reasons

Some of us cry because that's all we know how to do

Some of us cry because we're hungry or agitated

Some of us cry because our diaper needs to be changed

Some of us cry just because we want somebody to pick us up

Some of us cry because we want to feel someone else's heart beating against our own

Some of us cry just because we want attention from the people we love the most

After we become infants, slowly but surely, we turn into toddlers

We start crawling, walking, uttering words and getting into mischief

Before we know it, we start exploring and analyzing the things around us

And wanting to know what everything means and how things work

We began trying to put the pieces of the puzzle of life together

In whatever ways seems best or appropriate

Like young scientists, we eagerly search for answers

Of what this could mean, or what that could mean

Like sponges, we soak up everything we see, taste, touch, smell, hear, etc.

We began formulating valid as well as false perceptions

We start wondering what life is all about

And what position are we supposed to play in its realm

Some of us find our calling early on

While others aren't so fortunate

We become intrigued by the unknown aspects of life

And receptive to any lessons we may find appealing

Then there are other times when life's obscure or unmeaningful

And we still may partake in situations and circumstances that we can't fully comprehend

Yet we do so because it seems like the right thing to do

If there's anything I realize now, it is my mamma ain't raise no fool

I probably would've gone somewhere had I stayed in school

And obtained my education

I probably could've changed a nation or nations

And caused worldwide celebrations

While I wait for my blessings

I just practice being patient

And give thanks to my Lord for all His creations

Crystal Ball

Where does your treasure lie?

Is it financial gain that forces you to thrive?

Does having currency make you feel like you're alive?

Do you want to say more, yet sometimes swallow your pride?

Do you just go with the vibes?

What do you treasure most?

Is it your soulmate that never leaves your side?

Or is it your folks?

Maybe it's the friends you can always depend on?

When life surprises you with heartaches, twists, turns, and pitfalls

Are you still content when your pockets are full of lint balls?

Do you appreciate life less or more when you're not pissed off?

If only I were a psychic, and my paper was a crystal ball

Sometimes, I feel like I'm a Hebrew slave trapped in an Egyptian war

Remember

Remember how good it felt to receive your first VCR, cassette player, 8 track, or record player?

Remember your first pair of bell bottoms and your first butterfly collar shirt?

Remember when stores sold penny cookies and candies?

Remember growing up having pencil fights in school?

Remember going to pajama parties with all your classmates and friends from the neighborhood and from school?

Remember how it felt to be in love for the first time?

Remember being told you had to be home before the streetlights went on?

Remember being told never to hop in the car or take candy from strangers?

Remember how special it felt to hear your girl tell you she was pregnant with your child?

Remember how good it felt to win your first trophy for playing baseball, basketball, football, hockey, soccer, wrestling, or lacrosse?

Remember how special it felt to put on your first pair of Dr. Jays, British Walkers, Michael Jordans, Kobe Bryants, or LeBron James?

When We Were Poor

When we were poor, we had unity. Now look at our communities

Got nice cars, big houses, designer clothes, and big mouths

Everyone wants to do their own thing

And honestly, I can't blame anyone

Because life gave each and every one of us our own set of scars

We cover our scars with bandages

Live our lives like we're cancerous

We mock others who struggle with mental disadvantages

Instead of lifting one another up

We laugh as soon as we see someone fall

Some of us even think we're brainiacs

But what we won't admit is

No one knows it all

Besides the One who created us

And that's the Almighty Lord

I Don't Have Any Degrees

I don't have any degrees, and I don't know much about technology or how it works

But what I do know is this Earth was created for us to live on

Not for us to destroy and pollute

With all of these manmade chemicals, we're producing for financial gain

I wake up every day and ponder the thought of nuclear war occurring

And I find it very disturbing to imagine this world being destroyed

Nuclear warheads being released

By men in power that constantly shout, *We need to have peace!*

Yet never practice what they preach

The conclusion I've come to is that

We need to find better ways of dealing with our anger issues

Instead of resorting to bombs, military drones, and government missiles

Forgive and Forget?

Four hundred years of tears, and you expect us to forgive and forget

Still, to this day, I feel we were stripped

Robbed and raped, beaten with whips

Some of us were chained, others were lynched

Still, to this day, it doesn't make sense

How could you say, forgive and forget?

Blow the World Away

Bombs continued to explode as weapons began to unload

Mothers crying, innocent people dying, babies screaming

Families fleeing, seeking shelter on empty stomachs

Asking for government assistance

But what about our own district?

We have billions to send to other countries to fund wars

But back home, everybody's just tryinta to eat

I'm still waiting for Uncle Sam to clean up our streets

When are we gonna really focus on peace?

Let's find a solution to alleviate all of our grief

And provide people near and far with much needed relief

Before we blow the world away

We gotta practice what we preach

Switching Gears

At times, I feel like I'm trapped inside a prison cell

I hope I make it to Heaven

I'm tired of living in Hell

I lived in psychiatric centers, jails, motels and prison cells most of my life

I don't think I'm better than none of y'all

I chose to shake the dice

So, who am I to question God

For where He puts me?

My punishment's not so bad, and it's not like it's just me

I try my best to make do, stay true, and make ends meet

While painting pictures and switching gears with my verbal ten speed

As I let life continue to enrich me day by day

I tell my story and watch

As my atomic bomb blows half the world away

You see, there's not many things I haven't seen, heard, or dealt with

During the course of my life

I learned a lot from the experience

I even learnt that a sinful man can sometimes

Be the one who's in the right

Why?

If you're tired of fighting this ongoing battle, we're experiencing

Then learn to raise your voice to oppression and take my suggestions seriously

You see, you don't need to be aggressive in order to be heard

All you need to do is speak your mind, and people will respect your words

Because all around the world, there are people who are mentally disturbed

It's just many choose not to use their words wisely

So they end up being stigmatized or labeled as outcasts of society

However, I beg to differ because everybody's equal when you're looking at the bigger picture

There's really no right or wrong side to choose from

From New York, California, all the way back to Texas

We are all just living life, reaching out and preaching a message

I have so many questions of my own that just can't be answered

Like why allow people to smoke tobacco products

When all they do is cause cancer?

Or tell a man it's okay to have sex with another man?

That's just something I'll never understand

People teach others wrong and then expect them to do right

How many years will it take before a person decides to change their life?

We send supplies to other countries for people in need

But what about our own people who are homeless, living on the streets

With barely anything to eat

And squatting in buildings and houses

Why do we continue to sit back

Live life and watch in silence?

Why Do People Put Up Walls?

Why do people put up walls to hide who they really are?

It's the easier way to deal with life

Why do people put up walls to hide who they really are?

Because they don't want to deal with reality

Why do people put up walls to hide who they really are?

Because sometimes they're not comfortable in their own skin

Why do people put up walls to hide who they really are?

Because it hurts them too much to deal with the truth and be themselves

Why do people put up walls to hide who they really are?

Because maybe that's the only way they know how to deal with life

Greatest Ally, Worst Enemy

I'll break down the recipe for my greatest ally and my worst enemy:

It's time we woke up from this nightmare we've been living

We use substances in front of our children

Then, wonder how they'd become addicted

To crack, week, heroin, fentanyl, and cocaine

When it shouldn't take a mirror for us to see we're really to blame

We're quick to point our fingers at the drug dealers on the street corners

But aren't we just as guilty for misleading our own sons and daughters

And allowing our children to see us live our own lives so recklessly?

Throughout the years, I learnt I could be my greatest ally

And also my worst enemy

Say No to Drugs and Alcohol

Some people are tempted to try drugs and alcohol

Because they think it'll make them cool

But life is about growth and development,

So don't be another fool

Say no to drugs and alcohol,

While you're at it, stay in school

Learn to use your brain

Gotta outthink everybody else

And stay one step ahead of the game

You don't want to make the same mistakes

Myself and others made

If a friend asks you to drink or drug,

Say, "What are you, insane?"

Wake up before it's too late

'Cause in the long run,

All it's gonna do is cause you pain

If You Don't

If you choose to play the game

When something goes wrong, ain't no sense to complain

If you decide to take it to the next level

There's a strong possibility you'll find yourself in some serious trouble

If you sell your soul like Judas did for 30 pieces of silver

You'll pay the ultimate price in the afterlife

If you disobey the law and take matters into your own hands

You just might end up doing some hard time behind bars

And find yourself in a jam

If you think you know it all

And you're not openminded to advice and suggestions from others

You'll find yourself falling into a bottomless pit

If you don't decide what path of life you're going to choose

You'll live your entire life wandering aimlessly

Doing things you'll probably never forget

If You Want the Best Life Has to Offer

Instead of telling y'all lies

I'm going to leave y'all with some jewels

Drugs are everywhere

But that doesn't mean y'all have to use

Violence occurs every day

But y'all don't have to get involved

If you want the best life has to offer

You have to be willing to work hard

And get a job

Anyone can be a success story

It's all about what path you choose to travel

If you want to hit your mark

Sometimes, you have to aim as straight as an arrow

And last but not least, don't ever think narrow

Don't Let Others Influence You

Don't let others influence you to be someone you're not

If others want to try drugs, tell them to stop

Make up your mind not to get involved in crimes

And use the eyes God gave you to help lead the blind

Everyone has flaws and weaknesses they face

But in order to make it through each day, ask God to provide a little grace

Prayer goes a long way, and you'll never know what you'll get

If you fall short, all you need to do is get on your knees, repent and ask for forgiveness

Work on changing your lifestyle, and God will bear witness

Stay Sober, Remain Focused

I ain't joking when I say stay sober, remain focused

Use your mind, let it soar; that's what it was given for

You're talking to someone that almost did it all

But you don't need to be like me

Crawl before you walk

Don't try to be a centipede

Think before you utter your mind

Make plans to obtain the things you want out of life

If you're searching for answers, look toward the sky

We're all born with wings; it's just some of us haven't learned how to fly

Utilize your mind and hope for the best

When problems arise, cope with the stress

Drugs and Alternatives to Using

Don't ever think it's too late to stop because it's never too late

You can do it!

You just have to believe you can

The same way you picked up those drugs

You can put them down

But you have to be willing to make that commitment

There's nothing stopping you, but you

If you're tired of being broke and not having the things you want to have

Put the drugs down and watch how much money you save

It doesn't matter how long you've been using

You can quit if you want to

The choice is yours to make

Don't psych yourself out and tell yourself you can't

Because you can stop using it if you want to

If it takes you to change your surroundings, change your surroundings

If it takes you to change the crowd you're hanging around, change the crowd

Find an alternative to using

When you feel like using, get on your knees and pray

Read a book, go to AA, join a fitness club, talk to a friend

Take a walk, watch TV, listen to the radio, meditate

And if you have a successful day, find a sober way to celebrate

Spend quality time with your lover

Write about how you feel in your journal, go fishing

Get in your vehicle and take a long drive, go to the movies

Spend the money you used to spend on drugs

On your children or donate it to a charitable cause

Let's Rebuild

Let's pray that we make it to tomorrow, but keep the faith even if we don't

Let's mourn for our fallen soldiers in the streets and on the battlefields that weren't able to make it home

Let's rebuild the communities that drugs and alcohol continue to destroy

Let's create a magnetic workforce so people without jobs won't have to remain unemployed

Let's do away with welfare and focus our attention on building better healthcare systems globally

Let's stop being selfish and start offering our services to the homeless and helpless

Let's change the society we live in

And make the future brighter for not only our sons and daughters but the next generation of children

Life is Like a Chess Game

Life is like a chess game in so many ways

And the world we live in is kind of like a maze

The only difference is when dealing with life

We deal with more than sixty-four squares on a board

Life can teach us valuable lessons that we never thought we'd learn

Especially if we're not prepared

However, we need to be receptive, patient, and remember

No matter how long we suffer, our suffering won't last forever

In the Blink of an Eye

It's strange how your whole life can change in the blink of an eye

One minute, you're pouring your whole heart into something – the next minute, you're saying goodbye

In all actuality – there's really no telling what tomorrow will bring

Some find pots of gold – while others find diamond rings

In the blink of an eye – your whole life could come to a closure

Some people never chase their dreams – because they're afraid of exposure

While others grab the bull by the horns and ride their own emotional roller coasters

Who can actually predict – how their life will truly turn out in the end?

Some people are afraid to walk all alone – so they rely on their friends

Nobody knows how many ups and downs they'll experience – or how many times they'll sin

In the blink of an eye, everything you worked for – could be taken away

So the best advice I can offer – is to always pray, pray, and pray

Share Your Knowledge with the World

Climb up the mountains in your life

Stay humble when you reach the top of them

Love your brothers like you love yourself

Treat your sisters with respect

Seek wisdom every chance you get

Share your knowledge with the world

Teach your children better than you were taught

Love your neighbor

But When Is Enough Enough?

Life'll take you on journeys you don't want to take

What would happen if you woke up

And you had everything you ever wanted?

How would that make you feel?

Would you be satisfied?

Or would you still want more?

You know, people always say, *If I had this, I'd be happy*

But when is enough enough?

When does a man, woman or even a child become satisfied?

Show me a man, woman or child that has it all

And I guarantee they'll always want more

Life ◆ Stress ◆ Opportunity

Life will test you every chance it gets

So it's best to be prepared for whatever tomorrow brings

Stress is a part of life

Everybody deals with stress in one form or another

It's all about how you respond to the stress

Opportunity is somewhere lurking around the corner

You just have to hope you can see it when it presents itself

And in order to do that

First, you need to know what it looks like

Then, you'll be able to capitalize on your opportunity

When you see you have a chance to advance in life

Go for it and see where it takes you

That's Just the Way Life Is

Have you ever worked with somebody that seemed like they didn't want to see you get ahead?

Well, I have, and you know what it made me realize?

Some people just don't want to see others progressing

They'd rather see you struggling while they're advancing in life

I don't know why it's like that, but that's exactly how people are

And at first, it used to really bother me

But after giving it some serious time and thought

It made me realize

That's just the way life is

A True Friend

A true friend'll pick up the phone when you call for help

A true friend cares about others more than they care about themself

A true friend's love has no limitation

A true friend can make their friends feel amazing

A true friend loves everything they have

A true friend can make their friend smile even when they're sad

A true friend sticks by their friend's side even when the odds aren't in their favor

A true friend can warm the heart of a stranger

A true friend treats everyone like they're a neighbor

I Hope

I hope the Heavens can hear my cry

I hope that raindrops fall from the sky

I hope the hopeless person finds relief

I hope the hungry person finds something to eat

I hope the lost soul can find redirection

I hope that someday, everyone will appreciate their blessings

I hope the wars and ongoing fighting will stop

I hope one day, we'll have another peaceful march

I hope that all the bigotry will end

I hope someday, we can all turn away from our sins

I hope instead of us scheming on one another, we can all flourish and become friends

I hope someday my descendants and your descendants won't have disputes

But you know what I hope most of all?

That one day, we can live our lives based on Truth

The Way People Think

Have you ever felt like you've been chosen to perform a special task?

Are there times in your life you feel afraid, ashamed, or worried?

Do you wake up feeling exhausted even after you've slept for 8 hours straight?

The point I'm trying to make is no two people's answers are the same

Just like no two brains function the same

Everybody responds differently

You see, we all move at our own pace

Some of us are quick-witted when it comes to responding

And others aren't when it comes to responding

Then we have those that are in between

One of the things I've learnt is to never judge a book by its cover

And when I refer to books, I also mean people

Because both are full of surprises

What People Want

A blind man longs to see

An empty heart longs to be filled with love

A fool seeks wisdom to understand life

A precious life is worth more than diamonds, rubies, and pearls

A lost soul cries out from the gates of Hell

A lame mind wants to be understood

Deaf ears want to hear and be heard

Genuine love wants to be loved in return

A broken heart wants to be healed

A miserable person wants to find happiness and peace

A lost sheep awaits the arrival of the shepherd

A diseased body wants to be cured

A person in danger wants to be rescued

A hungry individual wants to be fed and nourished

A dreamer with a nightmare seeks relief

A captive wants to be set free

The holy plant their seeds on the righteous ground

The faithful are led by faith, not by sight

The spiritual see with the spiritual eye

Someday, I Hope

Someday, I hope to partake in a society made up of righteous people, both men and women, young and old, worshipping the highest Lord of all

Someday, I hope that all the leaders of this world can come together and find a common solution to alleviate all the problems we face

Someday, I hope that each man, woman and child can be given equal opportunities to pursue their dreams and aspirations and turn them into realities

Someday, I hope that men and women won't have to rob and steal to fill their bellies

Someday, I hope that the power of love can outweigh the value of gold and silver, and we can show lovingkindness to one another forevermore

Someday, I hope we can let go of our own selfish ways and share and embrace the true meaning of the bread of life that Christ once preached about

Someday, I hope all our sicknesses and physical ailments will be taken away from us and cast into the sea of forgetfulness, and we will be given new bodies to serve our Creator

Someday, I hope

Forks in the Road

If you say you can't see these forks in the road, you gotta be kidding

I hate to have to be the one to admit it

But from the beginning, we've been sinning

We're slaves to each of our own hidden pleasures

What may not entice one, another may look at as a treasure

And we're no better than one another, my sisters and brothers

We all have our own weaknesses and strengths

Some of us possess amounts of wisdom that constantly increase

While others aren't considered geniuses due to their own inner disbelief

We all make mistakes and live with regrets

But some of us act like we tend to forget

That's just the way life goes

And anyone who isn't on our side, we view as our foes

For some, it's difficult to make choices

When there are forks in the road

To Be the Best

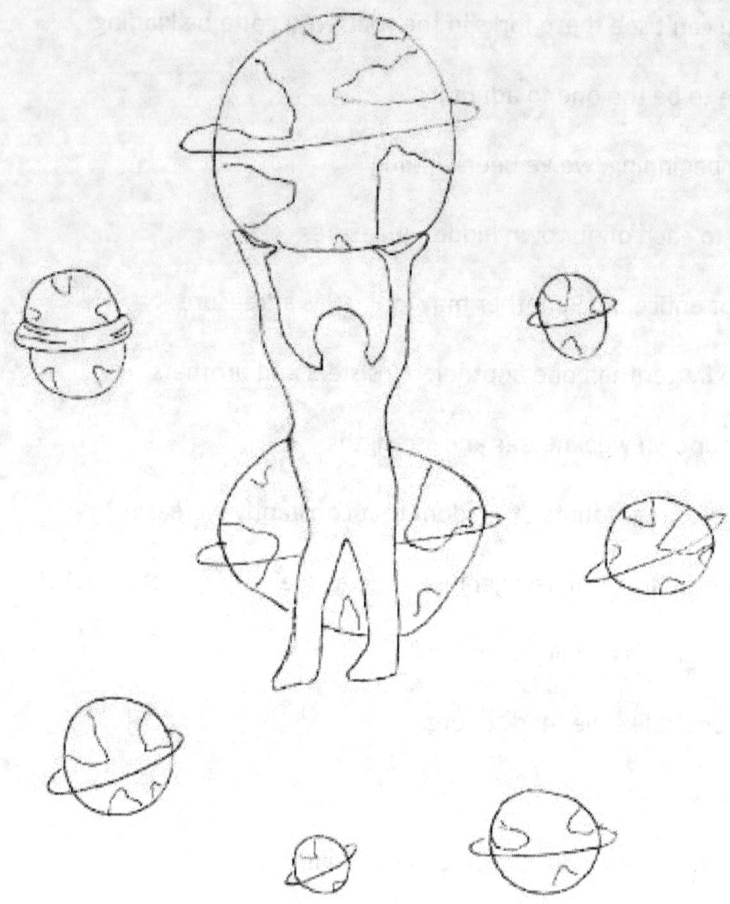

To be the best at what you do

It takes determination, practice, patience, and, most importantly, willpower

You need to be willing to go that extra mile

To obtain what you want out of life

Because believe me when I say

Nothing good comes easy

If you want it, you gotta work for it

Everything worth having takes an excessive amount of time to get

You gotta be willing to make sacrifices

Just to get what you want out of life

And sometimes, those sacrifices consist of working extra hours

In your home or in your office

Other times, in order to be the best

You might have to sacrifice some sleep and practice a little more often

Just so you could become better at what you do

For everybody, it's a different route to take

Your route and my route may be two totally different routes

However, the point I'm trying to make

Is that we all want to be the best

And in order to be the best

We need to stay committed

You Just Have to Be Patient

There's a rainbow somewhere out there

You just have to find it

There's a man or woman eagerly waiting to be found

You just have to keep searching for them

There's a job waiting for you

You just have to be willing to work

There's a mountain in your life that you can climb

You just have to have some faith with each step you take

There's a lonely soul reaching out to you

You just have to open your eyes in order to see who that person is

There's an opportunity right around the corner

You just have to look for it, and it won't pass you by

There's a powerful God that hears your prayers

You just have to be patient in order to receive your blessings

Keep Your Sights High

Stay in school, get your education

Plan ahead and practice being patient

Keep your sights high, don't focus on obtaining a reputation

Anyone can be a misfit, but you can be amazing

Do things differently, touch others' lives mentally

Strive to be great in all you do

And slowly watch all your dreams come true

Chase Your Dream

Don't let nobody stop you from being a dreamer

When you have a dream, chase it until you attain it

Even if it means you have to make sacrifices

Chase your dream

Don't let anyone stand in the way of accomplishing your goal

Know life is full of surprises

And no man's an island

No one can do it all alone

In a world full of surprises

Actors wear many disguises

To see what lies ahead

Search for your horizon

Believe in Yourself

Pick your head up, aim for the stars

Step your game up; life ain't all about cars

Open your eyes and accept your flaws

Nobody's perfect except the Lord

Don't just settle for less; search for your cause

Be all you can be, and act like the world is yours

Believe in yourself when everyone else chooses not to

And all the obstacles in your way,

Don't let any one of them stop you

Treasure Every Moment

Live life, love wholeheartedly, and treasure every moment you're given

Be optimistic, expect great outcomes at all times

Climb to new heights, embrace the challenges you face

Be courageous, eliminate self-doubt

Let your light shine so brightly that the darkness around you dissipates

Create a sanctuary within yourself that inspires continual growth

Allow peace and tranquillity to reside within your heart

Treasure every moment of the life you're given

And know that every day you're on Earth is a gift from God

DORI
NURSE ALTHEA W
LEX
THAESSA
VALERIE
LEVI
MICHELLE
MARJORIE
SHANEA
CHRISSY
JENNIFER
SHARIE
CK
FOR THE ♥ OF MONEY
JOLANTA
LAURA

NATEISHA
ANNMARIE
CARA
ANDREA
LYNNE
LYN
LIA
SONU
FU
FOR THE LOVE OF MONEY
LORIE
GABBY
TYLER
KARIN
WILLIE

KERRY ANN
TAONIE
JALEK
BINDYA
MARIANN
MO$
JOSHUA
KELLY
NATHALIA
MRS. DOLL
SAMUEL

ABOUT THE AUTHOR

Samuel Dickerson has survived and prevailed in the face of many life challenges, including physical injury, mental illness, substance abuse, incarceration, psychiatric hospitalization, heartbreak, and loss. Like an alchemist, he chooses to transform the "lead" of his experiences into "gold" through using creative arts for self-expression. In addition to poetry, he has written a large volume of gospel, R&B, and rap music lyrics. He draws cartoon characters, creates name art, and is in the process of making a series of comic books and clothing featuring his designs. He has spent years sculpting in various artistic mediums. He is in the process of designing an original board game. He recently published the book, *Inspirational Quotations*, featuring positive messages and artwork. Mr. Dickerson considers himself an entrepreneur and looks forward to making an honest living through selling and sharing his creations.

Mr. Dickerson is interested in hearing your feedback about his poetry and is open to future collaborations with other artists, writers, and thrivers.

Please write an Amazon review or contact:

SamDickerson010@gmail.com

998 Crooked Hill Rd.

West Brentwood, NY 11717

www.ingramcontent.com/pod-product-compliance
Lightning Source LLC
Chambersburg PA
CBHW080734120726
48001CB00009B/2579